Why Bother with

# THEOLOGY?

# Why Bother with
# THEOLOGY?

**Alex Wright**

DARTON · LONGMAN + TODD

First published in 2002 by
Darton, Longman and Todd Ltd
1 Spencer Court
140–142 Wandsworth High Street
London SW18 4JJ



ISBN 0–232–52409–2



A catalogue record for this book is available from the British Library.

The author and publisher gratefully acknowledge the following for permission to reproduce copyright material: Extract from *Duino Elegies* by Rainer Maria Rilke, translated by Stephen Mitchell, published by Vintage. Used by permission of Random House, Inc. Extracts from *The Magus* by John Fowles, published by Jonthan Cape. Used by permission of Sheil Land Associates Ltd. on behalf of J R Fowles Ltd. Extracts from *Falling* by Colin Thubron, published by Heinemann. Used by permission of Random House, Inc. Extracts from *A Change of Climate* by Hilary Mantel, published by Viking. Used by permission of the author.

Designed by Sandie Boccacci
Set in 10/13pt Palatino
Phototypeset by Intype London Ltd
Printed and bound in Great Britain by
The Bath Press, Bath

*To Alison*

# Contents

# Preface

When I was beginning to write this book I spent a week at my mother's Tudor townhouse in the very centre of Salisbury, one of southern England's greatest cathedral cities. Being a keen runner, I would jog the city's perimeter every evening after finishing work, taking in a route which included the Cathedral and its Close. There was the Cathedral, magnificent in its bulk, floodlit and glorious. Its fantastic spire reached heavenwards like a definitive appeal to divine involvement in human affairs, which, for all their provisionalities, could still give rise to this thing of exquisite beauty, this self-confident and self-proclamatory inspiration to countless worshippers over time. What, I wondered, did that building, with all its accumulated resonances, prayers and aspirations, actually represent today, both for me and for the community in whose life I was participating for those seven days?

It would be reassuring to be able to say that I was able to view the Cathedral as the centre of a community whose lives were directed, as they have been for centuries, by a power and authority greater than princes and principalities, founded on justice, and directed by the evenhanded outworkings of the Holy Spirit. It would be fine to be able to record that, for me, that building meant more than a symbol of something departed, something gone awry. But that would be disingenuous. The fact is that, as I pounded the tarmac of the Cathedral Close during those chilly February nights, while wondering at the astonishing ideals of those who conceived and then executed such magnificent architecture, I felt little but a sense of loss.

Like so many of our affluent southern historical towns, Salisbury conducts its affairs in the shadow of this great legacy, but without any sense of abiding ecclesial connection to its activities, other than viewing its cathedral as a convenient source of tourist income or as legitimation of a superior cultural heritage. Civic sensibility is thoroughly bound up with its shops, its cosmopolitan cafés, its bars and restaurants. Such sense of community as it has appears to be deeply located in this world, not associated with an eye to the next. Returning to Hackney from my holiday, I was reunited with the lively multi-ethnic and multicultural community of east London that is my home. Lacking the upper-middle-class affluence of Salisbury's citizens, but profoundly 'worldly' and self-confident and vibrant nevertheless, Hackney-ites are thoroughly immersed in a similar profusion of secular interests. And the same is true everywhere. Britain is the most radically secular country in Western Europe. How has Christianity in this country managed to marginalise itself so conclusively, so comprehensively, and so relatively quickly? What is to be done now that it has gone? Should we mourn its departure, or does this present us with fresh opportunities? What can theologians say about their discipline that can be given any credence in this climate? Above all, why should we bother with theology at all, in a society whose guiding principles are so thoroughly rooted in the here and now? These are some of the questions that I will be exploring and attempting to answer in this book.

Of course, it has to be strongly emphasised that I offer what are very much my own views on the questions, and that the questions are such that the answers given are hardly likely to be definitive ones. A word here should be said about method. At several points I make generalisations about the state of our society and culture that would not stand up to scrutiny in a thesis. The short, popular format of the book may be able to accommodate statements which attempt to be broadly representative, but which (I am well aware) are often quite subjective, and derive from the particular circumstances of the author. While it would have been possible to write about other manifestations of culture, such as architecture or contemporary art, I have decided to concentrate on literature and film. In the first place, books and films are central to my own interests, and, secondly, they seem to me to be as good a barometer for certain trends as any other significant cultural modes – or even, since they are genuinely 'populist', perhaps better. Furthermore, specific texts and films are cited which may appear to be rather selective and open to critical interrogation by my readers. While these are certainly the ones that I myself like best, they also seem to me to add up, collectively, to something hopeful for theological reflection and practice. In addition, I am quite sure that to many readers the book will not seem nearly theological enough. I am quite prepared to admit that whatever I say may well tell people more about the author than about God; but perhaps that is always the danger when addressing the ineffable and the mysterious.

In response to these several deficiencies, to which I readily admit, I can only apologise. In defence, I might say that the book is intended to bring a very personal perspective to bear on the main theme. Even if I had had the theological skills to bring to bear on the issues, a better-referenced and more 'academic' book would have been far longer, and in all likelihood more resistant to empathy from a popular audience. The absence of footnotes and a license to generalise are therefore deliberate. Perhaps lack of theological sophistication, and a certain forthrightness of style, may even be seen as virtues, in the case of a book which assumes that its readers may have lost interest in theology, and boldly seeks for them other points of reference. However, I should indicate that I would not have attempted to write the book at all if I did not think that the questions and answers were in themselves – and however ineptly – worth addressing.

I should also indicate that I do not think that the positive response to the question 'Why Bother with Theology?' is nearly so clear-cut as many contemporary theologians might think. Nevertheless, while the situation of the Church is certainly perilous, and while there is certainly no guarantee that others will be convinced by the answer 'Because it still matters', I do think that theology as a discipline, and as the programmatic articulation of the way of life and living to which it points, continues to have relevance within our society, for reasons which I will attempt to draw out. The marginalisation of the theological enterprise within contemporary Britain was for me graphically illustrated when every one of my non-theological friends answered the question, when it was put to them, by way of 'Why indeed?', or even 'Right: waste of time'. It is *that* comprehension of theology, if it is even thought about at all, as a monumental irrelevance to the business of living, which needs first to be tackled if any constructive defence is to be mounted. The fact is that people in the mainstream of British living are not interested in the Church and in what it once meant. Theology, as the time-honoured language of the Church – in effect the equivalent of Leeloo's 'divine language' in Luc Besson's film *The Fifth Element* – is as broadly incomprehensible today as are the hieroglyphs in the British Museum.

For those of us involved in the theological world, either as professional theologians, clerics, candidates for ordination, choirmasters, or the rump of believing laypeople, this should be seen as a challenge of self-definition, or even of self-justification, because we are a minority in an indifferent context. That context, as I have indicated, is overwhelmingly secular, but it is also, of course, pluralistic, multi-ethnic, and multi-faith. Only in institutionalised Christianity has the number of adherents plummeted to the point of virtual invisibility, and the statistics indicate that elsewhere, within other faith communities, the numbers of practising adherents are holding firm. More needs to be said about the relationship of Christianity to other religions in the UK, but that is not my main task here, and it would need another book to do justice to the topic. For historical and deep-rooted cultural reasons I take 'theology' to mean Christian theology; indeed, since relatively few Britons – 4.6 per cent – align themselves with religions other than Christianity, or set themselves apart from the 16.5 per cent of self-declared atheists and agnostics, I think this is probably justified on demographic grounds. Certainly we live in a thriving multicultural and heterogeneous society, but the fact is that a majority regard themselves as in some broad, though increasingly nebulous, sense to have some 'Christian' provenance. The point at issue is that, whatever our personal adherence, religion – predominantly Christianity – is now so thoroughly divorced from the public sphere that it is perceived to have become an irrelevant anachronism. Of the 65 per cent of adults who call themselves Christians fewer than 1 million regularly attend Sunday worship. In short, people don't go to church, they don't think about the Church, and by and large they operate as if there were no God. We, as theologians and churchpeople, might attempt to persuade ourselves that, for reasons of history and privilege, we can continue to exercise jurisdiction over those in our patch who are part of the larger majority. However, the legitimacy and sustainability of that activity must now be called into question. It seems to be the case that, despite calamitous decline, the churches will continue to exist in the form of some kind of sect, with ongoing commitment from decreasing numbers of communicants. But as the legacy of a once-powerful and dominant state-sponsored institution, this is hardly a very convincing or inspiring one.

As someone who has spent his whole professional life in the business of producing theological books, perhaps I have more at stake in this process of soul-searching than most. For if the soil is barren, then why go through the motions of watering it? There has to be a question here about the meaning and integrity of involvement in theological literature if its fundamental precepts are shaky: that is, if the subject's value and relevance to society at large are at the very least questionable. And it is perhaps the question of personal integrity that motivates me above all to get to grips with a manifesto on the margins. A few words about myself might be helpful at this point. I am not a churchgoer, though at school – since it was compulsory – I regularly participated in the ritual of Anglican worship. I am not confirmed or even baptised. My brother and I were brought up in a context, at least outside our various schools, of questioning agnosticism. I have nevertheless always been greatly interested in theology and religion, because only theology seemed – and still seems – to have a large and serious enough remit to get properly to grips with the meaning of life and the meaning of us. This interest culminated in a theology degree at Cambridge and latterly in four successive jobs publishing religious and theological books. Despite my continuing passion for the subject, or perhaps precisely because of it, I am well aware that my friends outside the guild regard me as something of an oddity. As far as they are concerned, theology is definitely not sexy. In the circles that I move in, where everyone is left-leaning, telling people that you publish books on theology for a living is a bit like revealing that you are a card-carrying member of the Conservative Party: in the aftermath of election wipeout in 2001, you might as well announce that you are a faintly curious leftover from another age.

It will be clear that I am dismayed by the lack of significance – seemingly ubiquitous – attributed to the metaphysical issues which I regard as fundamental to who and what we are, and that this dismay is another main motivator behind my project. I want to show that there may be life in theology yet, and that perhaps the metaphysical issues haven't gone away but have simply been translated into other contexts. If the resources for an intelligible theology are there, out in the world, then theology might usefully start looking for them. The daunting nature of this task was for me comprehensively revealed when, as I have indicated, I conducted my own straw poll, and not a single one of my friends was able to answer the question posed by this book in the affirmative. Nevertheless, I count myself fortunate that, in the last decade and a half, my involvement in publishing has brought me into contact with people who have very different backgrounds, ideals and aspirations from myself. So despite having had a highly privileged upper-middle-class upbringing and education, which I do not in any way denigrate, but which I do acknowledge as in some ways disadvantageous, I have been lucky enough to see the restrictive outlooks that might derive from such privilege widened and enhanced through alterity.

These overwhelmingly secular and de-religionised perspectives I have at all times found enriching, especially because I am convinced that it is *over there*, not, as it were, over here, that theology matters: that is, in the lives of those on the outside, rather than in the self-important pronouncements of church leaders, or (less usually) theologians, who believe that they have the answers. Theology divorced from reality in the here and now, which means our compromised, secularised, questioning reality, the reality of injustice and inequality, as well as the reality of the new day, in all its beauty and promise, devoid of religion or even apparently of God, is not in my view theology worthy of the word. What we are looking for, as I see it, in order for theology to matter, is a place where theology can be secular theology, and be recognised as such, in full legitimacy and authority. This is nothing more or less than an extension of Bonhoeffer's search for a 'religionless Christianity'. His famous question Who is Jesus Christ for us Today? is of all modern conundra the most profound and pertinent for us all, whether we be in Salisbury, Hackney, or Glasgow's Govan. There is no room on the sidelines for Augustine's Other City, as Philip Sheldrake has recently and rightly emphasised. If the Church is not *our* Church, the Church of the lost and the missing and the desperate, of the disenfranchised and the cynical, the non-believing and the indifferent, then it can be no kind of Church at all; it can be itself only and until 'it is broken open on behalf of the world in the midst of the world' (*Spaces for the Sacred*, p. 157). An exploration of what this might mean is what I hope to offer here.

In my father's house there are many rooms (John 14:2). Likewise, the imprint of many hands may be detected in the making of this book. My theological friends and authors have offered me much good fellowship and loyalty over the years, as well as excellent conversation, and I wish to single out in particular Gerard Loughlin, Colin Gunton, Chris Rowland, Graham Ward, Catherine Pickstock, Fergus Kerr, Peter Selby, Peter Sedgwick and Dan Hardy for their unfailing support, often through choppy waters. George Newlands, another old friend, made a number of perspicuous and helpful comments on the text, as did a former Cambridge supervisor, Graham Howes. I am very grateful to them both. I am grateful too to my editor at DLT, Katie Worrall, for her much-appreciated encouragement and for her implicit faith in my abilities. Stephen Pattison was a valuable interlocutor at an early stage, as were, at different times, Alex Stibbe and Spike Warwick. Other friends have generously tolerated my theological eccentricities, and I have benefited greatly from their ready eagerness to talk of other things, which – perhaps unbeknownst to several of them – have directly or indirectly influenced my ideas as they now appear here. Laurence Hallam, John Bunney, Linda Thomas, Karin Azzopardi, Sarah Kett and Jenny Willis are the drinking partners concerned. Meanwhile, my old partners in crime at SPCK, Naomi Starkey and Rachel Boulding, have demonstrated the real meaning of Christian fellowship, especially over lunch. My present colleague Anna Hardman made many acute and valuable observations on the text, from which I have greatly benefited. My mother lent me her house in order to kick-start the book into action, and gave support in many other ways, while Tom and Rachel Lawson repeatedly offered most generous hospitality, and thinking space, at Christmas times.

Finally, Ian, Zoë, Harry and Bertie epitomised the value of cheerful community in a manner that was generously inclusive – even after the best man's speech!

I dedicate this book to Alison Lawson, who in her various ways has been a terrific friend and inspiration over the years, in the possibly vain hope that it might for a few hours tempt her away from the competing and undeniably superior attractions of *Inferno*.

# CHAPTER 1

# Outlining the Problem

Theologians sometimes speak about our culture of post-modernity as the culture of death, or one in which it is not so surprising that such a designation should be made, given the gulf between our fallen world and that of the redeemed world to come when Christ returns to rule in glory. But dogma aside for a moment, it is worth asking how the culture of this nation could change so quickly and decisively from one where, in the 1950s, 'religion mattered and mattered deeply in British society as a whole' (Brown, *The Death of Christian Britain*, p. 7) to one where we are approaching meltdown, and the established churches are perched on the edge of the ravine. The same commentator conceives of Britain as a highly religious nation up until at least 1963, after which tried and tested infrastructures, both cultural and institutional, began to disintegrate. The consequences are now apocalyptic:

> In the year 2000 less than 8 per cent of people attend Sunday worship in any week, less than a quarter are members of any church, and fewer than a tenth of children attend a Sunday school. Fewer than half of couples get married in church, and about a third of couples cohabit without marriage. In England only a fifth of babies get baptised in the Church of England, and in Scotland one estimate is that about a fifth are baptised in either the Church of Scotland or the Roman Catholic

> Church. By some calculations, as few as 3 per cent of people regularly attend church in some counties of England, and in most the non-churchgoers represent over 90 per cent of the population. If church participation is falling, all the figures for Christian affiliation are at their lowest point in recorded history. Christian church membership accounts for less than 12 per cent of the people and is falling. There is now a severe crisis of Christian associational activity: religious voluntary organisations, which formerly mushroomed around congregations and independent missions, account for a minuscule fraction of recreational activities. Most critical is the emerging evidence of the decay of Christian belief. Though 74 per cent of people express a belief in the existence of some kind of God or 'higher power', 50 per cent or fewer subscribe to the existence of sin, the soul, heaven, hell or life after death while the numbers having specific faith in Jesus Christ as the risen Lord are considered so statistically insignificant that opinion pollsters do not even ask the question. (Brown, p. 4)

Indicative of erosion and secularisation in this picture are some well-known cultural moments: Penguin Books' trial over publication of *Lady Chatterley's Lover* (1967); the legalisation of abortion (1967); the capacity to obtain easier divorce; the emergence of women's lib from 1968 onwards; the rise of youth culture, especially articulated through pop music (particularly following the impact of the Beatles in 1962); and student revolt, especially from 1968 through the early seventies. Public concerns have undergone a sea-change since the 1960s, during which time ethical issues such as care for the environment, feminism, nuclear weapons and power, holistic well-being and vegetarianism have dominated moral culture in such a way that Christianity is seen to be wholly unrelated to them. At the same time, 'the social implications of conventional religious culture – respectability, sobriety, observance of social convention, observance of the sabbath – have been rejected *en bloc*. Even where a moral goal appears to have survived (as with sobriety, especially in relation to driving), this has been remoralised in discourse in a form completely divorced from religiosity and Christian ethics' (Brown, p. 190). The really decisive factor in the demise of British Christianity, for Callum Brown, is that for young women and girls there is no longer any moral identity or femininity to be affirmed at church, and it is women, not men, who from 1800 have constituted the gender majority there. The result is a search for personal faith in the alternative directions, attractive to significant numbers of women, of consumerism, New Age philosophy, and personal development. Although such a facet of church decline is under-explored by Brown, the ubiquity in women's magazines of the myriad concerns that could be broadly designated 'holistic', as well as the determination with which self-help and self-development issues are promoted in particular to women, are factors which appear to bolster his claim.

This predominantly socio-historical and sociological account, informed also by some gender theory, paints a lurid portrait of Christian culture in its death throes at the end of the last century, which will be all too recognisable to those prepared to acknowledge that this culture, in its current form, has had its day. However, one of the major deficiencies of Brown's otherwise useful and hard-hitting analysis is that he fails to give enough attention to quite to what degree the churches (and those other harbingers of the Christian message) have been instruments of their own demise. It is not just that they have been overwhelmed by eventualities, social and cultural currents, and other demographic setbacks altogether outside of their own control. Clearly the imperative towards secularisation and consequent loss of authority has been a difficult one to counter; but there have been other factors which have been well within their own spheres of responsibility, and which have indicated in the clearest possible manner that – excepting some pockets of enlightenment – they have not been adequate or responsible custodians of the message that they profess to bear. It should be emphasised that decline is certainly not the case in every religious context. Whichever religion we profess, our landscape is an all-encompassing secular one, yet 63 per cent of those who align themselves with non-Christian religions say that they actively practise their faith, compared with a minimalist 23 per cent of those who identify themselves as practising Anglicans (Yates, *Britain Uncovered*).

Christianity speaks of the availability of salvation for all humankind if this fallen humanity stakes its hopes on the salvific actions of God's messenger and Son, Jesus the Christ ('this is the work of God, that you believe in him who he has sent' – John 6:29), who came into the world in order to change the malignant imperative of the created order by way of his death by crucifixion, subsequent resurrection, and ascension into heaven. These events are life-changing to the degree that those who accept the risen Christ as Lord, and repent truly of their sins, are promised a place at the right hand of the Father upon death. Furthermore, the Book of Revelation indicates a time when those who still inhabit the earth will see the return of Christ in glory, when all tears will be wiped away, and universal justice and peace will prevail on a planet whose redemption will at last materialise. The wicked will be judged; the repentant will join the angels in heaven; all will be reconciled, for better or worse, into God. In the meantime, the beneficent activities of the Holy Spirit help sustain the community of believers, in all its aspects, until the End.

Such a message, the bare bones of all the vast corpus of doctrine that makes up the repository of the Church's teaching, preaching and reflection, is so extraordinary and transformational a story, that it is hard to understand how it could be rendered inaudible by the trammels of secular life – if, that is, it is actually true. But it seems this is where we now stand, in the secular West, and particularly in Christian-less Britain, the acme of agnosticism or self-absorbed interiority. We are in a place where the predominant noises to be heard are those of mobile phones warbling in shopping arcades, where everybody talks but few listen; and where people strive for a feeling of connectedness to something bigger and more significant than themselves, and yet are left unsatisfied by a regiment of Nokia dialling tones. Grace Davie, who regards religion in Europe as a form of collective memory (and sees modern Europeans as amnesiacs, or those who are no longer *capable* of maintaining the memories that used to underlie their religious existence), notes that 'A marked falling-off in religious attendance . . . has not yet resulted in a parallel abdication of religious belief' (*Religion in Modern Europe*, p. 8). Likewise, I would suggest forcefully that people are as interested in religious and theological issues as they ever were, but that their needs and anxieties have been neglected woefully by a Church that has lost touch with how to communicate what is most important to us, and what is most crucial to it. And that missing component is a workable and credible narrative for life.

The Bible contains a story which is supposed to be the bedrock of all our individual stories: a story of sacrifice, betrayal, death and hope for redemption – ground zero for the whole human condition. It offers a paradigm not only for how to live our lives in dignity and truth (especially the letters of Paul and the Sermon on the Mount), but also of how to prepare ourselves for death, viewed not as any kind of definitive state but merely as a stage of transition from one mode of being to another. The New Testament has been the single most important handbook in the process of constructing the social, cultural and historical infrastructure of this country. The majority of our social and cultural mores, as well as many of our institutions, laws, architecture, and civic processes are directly attributable to what the Church has propounded on the basis of that text. It is hard to accept that in the space of thirty to forty years, because the impulses behind secularisation have supposedly reached a critical mass, and a trickle has turned into a flash flood, all of this masonry, the fabric of our civilisation, has crumbled and floated away downstream – a process as sudden as it is irrevocable. Certainly those points of meaningful connection between Church and society have to my mind been lost, but I would not propose therefore that the traditional foci of theological and religious reflection have disappeared also. It is rather a question of reconnecting Church – understood as the community of God – to civic life, in such a manner as to re-energise the reciprocal processes that undergird the foundations of our society.

How then has the battery gone flat? In the first place, church leaders have failed to respond in intelligible, sensitive language to the suspicions, fears and cynicisms of a generation that has learned how to question established givens and, indeed, the veracity and authority of the Establishment itself. The story of the dying and rising God made plenty of sense in the context of the first-century ancient Near East, with its immersion in the agrarian rites of the seasons, its familiarity with the cultic stories of bounty, sowing and reaping, and its resonance with the sacrificial deity who through self-immolation makes good the harvest. Such language has continued to resonate through history, especially in rural societies, though even so eventually convinced a Christian as the converted C. S. Lewis could lament that Norse mythology and pagan stories initially did so much more for him than study of the Bible (see Carpenter, *The Inklings*, p. 7). The particularities of culture, and the difficulties of mediating the truths of one age to another, when the contexts and points of reference have changed, even those which are supposedly universal truths, are not confined just to our own time.

Alain de Botton in his book *The Consolations of Philosophy* draws attention to just this point: 'Every society has notions of what one should believe and how one should behave in order to avoid suspicion and unpopularity . . . If common sense is cordoned off from questions, it is because its judgements are deemed plainly too sensible to be the objects of scrutiny' (p. 9). Thus, contemporaries of Socrates 'would have been confounded and angered to be asked exactly why they sacrificed cocks to Asclepius or why men needed to kill to be virtuous. It would have appeared as obtuse as wondering why spring followed winter or why ice was cold' (p. 13). The difference between ancient Athens and our own society is that in ours there is a clear sense of disjuncture between what an older generation thinks about tradition and religion and what is considered normative by the young. The whole of Athens was shocked at the desecration of the herms (or sacred civic idols), prior to its fleet's departure for the invasion of Sicily. But I would suggest that to be seen reading a Bible today on a train or bus, if you are under thirty, or even forty, is the equivalent of cultural death. Conversely, Church censure of club and drug culture is as intellectually incomprehensible to most of Britain's youth as is the proclamation that God died for our sins on a cross two thousand years ago. Within society there is no longer any real sense of homogeneity, of shared values, of goals, or even of identity. Cultural commentators Miranda Sawyer and Nik Cohn have both written entertaining and spirited books recently about this acute sense of dislocation and diversification in contemporary Britain, and it is by no means clear, from the stories and anecdotes related in *Park and Ride* and *Yes We Have No*, whether one can in any way generalise about the state of the nation, such is its plurality, fragmentedness and overwhelming confusion. 'Is this a nation, a way of life, saying farewell to itself?' asks Cohn:

> The brief answer was Yes. The old England was indeed dead or dying. Stability was gone; so was the sense of certainty. Despite the bromides of Tony Blair and his Cool Britannia cheerleaders, this was now a land full of trouble, violent and dispossessed, in some places close to anarchy . . . And against all that, there was what? Passion, energy, humour, rage. (p. xv)

Sawyer, meanwhile, writing with sharp wit and attractive self-deprecation about the essentially disintegrating boundaries between the urban and suburban, observes that:

> I didn't move to suburbia because, in the end, I didn't need to. Suburbia had moved to me. I had left but it had followed. I couldn't escape, even when I wore stupid clothes or listened to strange music, even when I hid. Run to Manchester, or London, hole up in city drinking holes, scum-soaked gutters, Soho-boho-hooligan art quarters; hunker down with the glamorous, the intellectual, the scary, the disenfranchised, the dangerous, the iconoclastic and still you'll find you're there. Because the only way that cities can compete with suburbia nowadays is to turn themselves into the same experience. Pedestrianise, cobble over, clean up, sanitise; provide decent toilets and crested litter bins and vast, safe parking areas. (p. 307)

Just because it is difficult to convey universal truths or instructive insights from one context or generation to another, or to speak meaningfully in an age where social and cultural fragmentation abounds, does not necessarily make the task less vital. And it is the prevalent conservatism of much of church life – jarring uncomfortably and anachronistically with an observation made elsewhere by Miranda Sawyer that 'we are all more complex, more tricky and wayward and human than any classification could ever reveal' ('Don't Fence Us In', *Britain Uncovered*) – that makes its attempts at communication so ineffectual and so sporadic. Partly this is a problem about language: the Church's vocabulary is hopelessly out of phase with that of the people and lives to which its message is directed. It fails to see that its conceptuality needs to cohere with what people are realistically likely to be able to understand in an age of multiple distraction and contextual dissonance. Above all, its liturgical practices seem both uninviting and impenetrable. But there is a deeper problem, beyond individual words or rites. There is a fundamental lack of *strategic* imagination about how to communicate effectively with those who are still concerned with exactly the fundamentals that preoccupied Jesus. Yet, since these are human fundamentals, such as meaning and identity, status, corruption, hypocrisy, guilt and forgiveness, they preoccupy us all.

Even an initiative judged relatively successful, such as the Alpha Course (which, run out of Holy Trinity Church in Brompton, has for the last decade articulated a popular, evangelical vision of Christianity), tends to gloss over cultural, class and social differentiation in its attempt to provide what some have described as a kind of evangelical McDonalds. While Alpha's appeal to the contemporary is in one sense admirable, it has relatively little awareness of what the contemporary might mean outside of middle England. Founded and run by those in high society, and lacking – as so much evangelical theology tends to – a clear socio-political agenda, Alpha, in the words of Stephen Hunt, 'appears merely to add to the middle-class cohorts of the charismatic movement' (*Anyone for Alpha?*, p. 116). A more disparaging view is that this is Christianity for yuppies. Its tendency to dumb things down, furthermore, 'means that the Alpha programme sets and answers its own questions. It over-simplifies sophisticated critiques of Christianity and then destroys them. It allows little discussion of the complex issues. It is, then, in its own way, hermetically foolproof' (Hunt, p. 112). Alpha, in other words, sets out to answer the questions before it asks them, and then give the answers to those who are predominantly affluent and already well educated. The result is that, despite the attention it has received, it 'probably is not winning a substantial number of new converts' (p. 113). I would propose that fundamentally a lack of genuine empathy, understanding or moral courage characterises much of what goes in the Church of England. There is a bunker mentality which gets in the way of connecting sensitively or with integrity with the affairs of people at large, especially those on the margins and young people. Concomitantly, these constituencies are not – or feel that they are not – taken seriously, even though young people naturally think that their cultural life is the most serious thing that there is.

My own experiences of many clergy in the Anglican Church is that they seem hopelessly out of touch with society *out there*, but appear to have no sense either that this is the case or, if they do – even worse – that this is a deficiency worth addressing. This detachment is especially noticeable in matters of business and sex. In matters of business (where certain standards of professionalism are elsewhere assumed as a given), amateurism and paternalism are frequently conspicuous, from one Christian-run institution to another. As a result of serious miscalculations, the Church is now in deep trouble with its pensions policy. It may have to sell off up to half its assets to pay clergy pensions, having already seen £800 million wiped off the value of its investments following its Commissioners' disastrous property speculations in the 1980s. As for matters of sexuality, either pious generalisations or a reluctance to engage at any meaningful level with individual people's real situations are the prevalent disposition. Even worse than detachment is hypocrisy. The sexual scandals which have rocked the Church establishment in recent years, especially the Roman Catholic Church in Britain, have hardly helped to bolster its credentials for sensitive and humane engagement with the sorts of problems that characterise day-to-day life in the world.

On top of this is the institutional prejudice that ostracised and discriminated against women for generations (Anglican women still may not be installed as bishops, and Catholic women seem as far away from winning the right to be ordained to the priesthood as they have ever been), and that now discriminates against gay and lesbian people. The debates of the 1998 Lambeth Conference were regarded as a major setback to the cause of homosexual emancipation and equality in the Church, and their outcome was thematically foreshadowed by Antonia Bird's striking and brave film *Priest* (1994). Even while arguably it packs a few too many social problems into its two fast-paced hours, the movie powerfully and movingly indicates just how retrograde, rigid and repressive ecclesiastical socio-sexual polity can be.

There is a sense that ecclesiastical Britain has lost touch with what it ought to be there for: to preach good news to the poor and maimed and blind and lame – in the Russian filmmaker Andrei Tarkovsky's parlance, 'the wretched'. Or, as Cohn pungently describes them, 'the jobless, the homeless, the fucked. The vast masses banged up in tower blocks and housing estates . . . Caribbeans and Irish, Africans and East Europeans, and their children, British-born, who were the new English . . . Born-agains, bikers, fetishists, faith healers, visionaries, squatters, druggies, lunatics, and street heroes' (p. xv). The Church rarely seems to have a connection with its own constituencies, with the people beyond the cathedral close. It is more concerned with contemplating its own internal affairs, or with issuing opaque and vacuous statements about how 'we live together in God's creation'. The recent incapacity of the Anglican hierarchy to make a firm recommendation to voters in the 2001 general election was entirely consistent with its general outlook. There are of course some notable exceptions, such as Kenneth Leech, who is still able to ask 'How am I to make creative sense of all this anger, despair and pain which surrounds me and all who work in the inner areas?' (*The Eye of the Storm*, p. 129), but they seem disproportionately thin on the ground, and as Leech acknowledges himself, context – in his particular case, Aldgate, East London – is all.

Religious publishers often collude with this determinant church culture of conservatism, and it is marked how few publishers' catalogues are concerned, in their publishing, with the concrete problems and debates of life as it is lived in the here and now. Theology, if it is worth anything at all, surely ought to be engaged with precisely these issues of contemporary secular life and thought: with sex; poverty; inequality; race; ethnic plurality and multiculturalism; gender; politics; economics; technology, and so on. But what tends to predominate in religious publishing (at least in the catalogues of most 'confessional' religious presses: by and large I exempt the secular presses, who are paradoxically – but not so surprisingly – rather less conservative, given their commitment to all sorts of academic endeavour) are books by churchpeople addressed, it seems, to churchpeople, bypassing the world outside the cloister. This introversion is paralleled by many of the specialist religious bookshops that stock this material. Especially in our smaller towns and cities, these appear to be stranded in a timewarp, exuding the musty atmosphere and censorious moral climate of the 1950s.

Few theologians are, any longer, pastorally or ecclesiastically influential, and their voices are too little heard outside the universities and secular institutions in which they are located. Often marginalised within their secular institutions, administratively overstretched, and too often under pressure to justify their own existence, they are likewise dislocated from the clergy who no longer read or have the capacity to empathise with what they are doing. The result is a disconnection between church life and the theological lifeblood that ought to be energising and powering it. It has been observed that clerics who do not read theology are like doctors practising medicine without ever referring to the *BMJ*. The latter scenario is certainly alarming – at least it is to me – but in its ramifications perhaps the former is in its own way just as damaging. For most people Easter is mainly about chocolate eggs and a long weekend while Christmas is mostly about babies and presents; but what else? Ask the man or woman on the street in Dalston or Clapton to name it, and I wager you will be waiting some time. I suspect the stumbling block to its continued reception is that too much theology is perceived as being too dull or too obscure to be intelligible or interesting to those who are most in need of it: the practitioners at the sharp end in the parish – the deacons, vicars, and churchwardens; the youth leaders and convenors of Bible study groups; the 'godfearers' who yearn for something fulfilling and intellectually satisfying that goes beyond the merely platitudinous, or the tediously sentimental and breezily pious.

The vacuum that exists in meaningful contemporary theological discourse, in God-talk, is characterised by the attention that often has been afforded to those theologians who represent extremes in their positions, and by the corresponding decline in the influence of what is usually called liberal theology. On the one hand, anti-realist thinkers like Don Cupitt – formerly Dean of Emmanuel College in Cambridge – famously abandoned objective theism (in his case even while an ordained minister of the C. of E. – which added to the sense of outrage and opprobrium). Partly they perceived there to be too many inconsistencies in the realist acceptance of traditional Christian doctrines, but also they found that notions of divinity made sense only when understood as the equivalent of the human religious consciousness. That is, God is not above or around us, but in us: in fact, conceived collectively, he *is* us. Such a position, while certainly an ingenious response to the agnosticism and sense of ennui in much contemporary life, is hardly an adequate comeback to the very real religious and theological needs of people at large. Essentially a sort of sanitised Christian neoplatonism, arguably it offers little more than a psychological explanation for our religious impulses – or a cultural placebo for spiritual nourishment – and can therefore seem both experientially shallow and overly intellectual to its detractors. There is no doubt that it has provided a safe haven for many Christians who have found themselves disillusioned with what they regard as the incredible supernaturalism of much theology. Perhaps, however, the continuing attractions of the Sea of Faith Network (so-called after the book and TV series of that name written and presented by Cupitt) come down finally to the sympathetic appraisal offered recently by Richard Holloway: that it 'celebrates the diversity of the meanings we devise for ourselves in our search for understanding' ('Mixed Bathing in the Sea of Faith', *Time and Tide*, p. 69).

On the other hand, the home-grown theological movement which in recent years has captured something of the same public interest as that of Cupitt and his followers is Radical Orthodoxy, whose main practitioners are Graham Ward, John Milbank and Catherine Pickstock. The term 'radical' suggests a progressiveness of outlook but in this sense it would be misleading. In the way it is used by the radical orthodox, the word refers to the *radix*, the root, of Christian doctrines and beliefs, with a view to the recovery of their fundamentals. These may thus be re-energised for church life in the midst of what is designated by them the 'culture of death', in other words the destructive culture of capitalism and postmodernity in the late twentieth and early twenty-first century. This is, then, a quest for a pure, unpolluted form of Christianity. In its high-Church Anglicanism, its affinity with Catholicism, its reliance on a manifesto or a series of programmatic publications, and its reaction against what it sees as an overarching and negative cultural hegemony, it shares many affinities with prior religious or semi-religious groups like the Oxford Movement and the Pre-Raphaelite Brotherhood. The supposedly heretical theories of the secular social sciences and the nihilistic theologies that have predominated in the post-medieval West are rejected. The radical orthodox – especially John Milbank and Catherine Pickstock, in their respective books *Theology and Social Theory* and *After Writing* – retrieve, from Augustine and Aquinas in particular, the resources which they see as necessary to conceptualise the true Church. This is a church that finds harmony and fulfilment in the Trinity, in worship, in music, and in liturgy. Above all, it is a church that utterly rejects the long-term validity of the secular context in which it temporarily resides (or with which it sits side by side): at the end of time, secular modernity will be seen as but a blip in God's plan for humanity, where everything is taken up and reconciled to Christian doctrine. The problems inherent in this position are as follows. It can be accused of appealing only to an intellectual elite; of failing to comprehend the nature of reality; of being utopian and conservative; of writing off the secular world with panache but with little compassionate insight into the possible value of resources other than Christian ones; and of sublimating the here and now to a future time when all will be made whole, thereby single-handedly giving fresh legitimacy to the whole phenomenon of liberation theology.

To be fair, a number of the recent writings of Graham Ward – sometimes seen as being the most culturally literate and open-minded of the three – have pointed towards a much more nuanced and inclusive set of theological positions than the earliest statements of the movement seemed ready to countenance. In his book *Cities of God*, Ward writes that:

> Christian theology cannot renounce the secular world on two counts. First, it cannot do so theologically: its teachings on creation and incarnation stand opposed to such Manichaeanism. Secondly, it cannot do so sociologically: Christians are part of the secular world, they work in it, with it, and buy the goods. They too are taken in by and foster the demands of the global market. Furthermore, the retreats to fundamentalism and neo-conservatism do not redeem the secular. They do not therefore bring healing, salvation, and the conviction of what is sinful and what is good. They just leave the secular to rot, retreating into privatised communities. (p. 69)

This is encouraging. Nevertheless, some of the inconsistencies in the movement's programme have been taken to indicate that it may not hold together for much longer in the form in which it came into being. For the moment, however, it certainly remains the most vital and energetic grouping on the British theological scene, despite an apparent reluctance, at least from some of its members, to consider an earthly – as opposed to an other-worldly – church operating with legitimacy and freedom of movement within what is portrayed as an unredeemed, violent and manifestly unpleasant world. In the meantime, the lack of a publicly understood theology that engages clearly and unambiguously with the lives of real people is the most notable absence on the contemporary stage. Although there is a rich history of liberal theology in Britain, the theologians who have come to be seen as representative of that position are far less influential than they once were. Many find this development demoralising, given the determination of these individuals to embrace modernity, to face up to the challenges of natural science, biology and Darwin, empiricism, and the aggressive critiques of atheists such as Richard Dawkins, and to argue for the merits of Christianity on terms set by others. Their decline in some respects mirrors that of the old Liberal Party, squeezed between two opposing forces both adopting more vociferous and more polarised positions than themselves, in this case Cupitt and the out-and-out secularists on the doctrinal left-wing, and an (unholy) alliance of evangelicals and radical orthodox on the right-wing.

Certainly there are a few important theologians who adopt a sort of third way, between liberalism and radical orthodoxy. They wish to get to grips with contemporary culture, and to try to make sense of the Christian message in such a way as to point to viable ways forward for their work and discipline, but without jettisoning the value of much of secular discourse. I will be looking at the work of some of these theologians – I call them 'cultural theologians' – in a later chapter. But for the most part, theologians seem reluctant to acknowledge legitimacy and truth other than where it is found in biblical authority, canon law and Church doctrine. The consequences are that theology can often seem as out of touch as the social and sexual morality of church leaders. Those church officers are thus left without precisely the resources that they need in order to make sense of society today, with the still further ramification that nobody cares or in fact knows about what Christianity may have to contribute to the constructive ordering of our world. There is a domino effect whose knock-down leads to theological marginalisation at every stratum of existence. It is not just the onrushing tide of secularisation that is to blame for the decline of Christianity in this country. It is also a phenomenon directly attributable to the absence of theological inspiration and leadership; to the disinclination to engage with a 'postmodern' culture that has become detached from traditional givens and accepted norms; to a continuing adherence to paternalism and patronage, where key appointments can be made on the basis of who knows who on which church committee, rather than on grounds of genuine ability; to embarrassment about sex and a reluctance to accept the disintegration of previously sanctioned modes of personal relationship; to different sorts of morality and differently understood codes of ethical practice.

The effect is that theology retreats either into pious platitudes which nobody other than conservative churchmen want to hear, or else into abstruse semantic hair-splitting, which only those possessing postgraduate degrees in a very dense and complex form of traditional systematic theology (taking its inspiration particularly from Karl Barth's critique of modernity) will be likely to comprehend. What theology needs to do is to reconnect with both Church and world; then it will speak with a new authority and a demonstrable relevance. In order to do this, it must open its eyes to the condition of postmodernity and must in fact get to know it as a fellow traveller – not as an enemy or a usurper – from which it has much to learn along the way. Despite its contemplative side, theology traditionally has been a didactic discipline, preaching and lecturing to others. What it now needs to rediscover is the capacity to listen – the capacity for silence. Such a theology will be empathic and open-minded and respectful. It will recognise what it sees as being wholly legitimate repositories of wisdom, and that these are often as invigorating and rejuvenating as its own. Above all, it needs to take on board that, by itself, it does not have all the answers; a process of reciprocal exchange is necessary in order for Church and world to make sense to one another. Like Titus departing Gormenghast, theology needs to take its leave of its ancestral home and find another country; one that is just as strange, but far from cobwebbed and redundant, and full of enriching possibility.

In the end, it may be God's will that Christianity is to die out in the secular West. If that is so, it takes nothing away from the power, wisdom and integrity of that will, or of its capacity to provide refreshing alternatives. Daniel Hardy has written of Christian faith as being by its nature '*spread out*, as something *extended* by its "spread-out-ness" ' (*Finding the Church*, p. 110).

This characteristic, what he calls 'extensity', embraces a living process of history, where divine wisdom comes to us in the course of time and through many different lives, as well as from the rainbow disciplines: from across the whole range of humanities and social sciences, rather than just 'concentrations of Christian faith in Bible, Church, beliefs and certainties' (ibid.). In later chapters I will explore in more detail how this 'wisdom theology' might look, and how the capacity for knowledge and articulation of God – what instead I call 'secular theology' – might be mediated to us. In the next chapter I will look more directly at our condition of postmodernity, how this has come about, and how it has affected the way we in Britain think or do not think about matters of transcendence and religiosity. I will examine some of the ways in which the culture of millennial capitalism threatens to consume us, and what the consequences, for good and ill, of rampant secular capitalism might be. In the third chapter I will show how British religious thinking, where it manifests itself explicitly, increasingly has broken free of established Church boundaries, and has relocated to resources provided by the New Age and that corpus of thinking and literature which has come to be designated 'mind, body and spirit'. As we will see, there is in that thinking much that is inconsequential, in comparison to Christian doctrine. However, we will discover also how much there is in mind, body, spirit (MBS) literature which points to truths that are universal and that are indicative of an immense interest in spirituality and the inner life. Certainly there seems to be quite a bit more to this thinking than most Christian theologians have generally been prepared to admit.

# CHAPTER 2

# Postmodernity

In the United Kingdom today society is pluralistic, fragmented and uncertain. You can go to the building society in a coffee shop – or sit and sip cappuccino in a building society. You can take out a mortgage in a supermarket. You can manage your bank account, or even go dating, on-line. You can watch a video on your computer screen, make phone calls from your personal handset to anywhere in the world, and – if, like me, you live in Hackney – eat dinner in a restaurant that has been converted from a church. As far as religion goes, you have a vague notion of wanting to 'explore your spirituality' or 'develop your inner life', though you have little desire to resort to the unattractively authoritarian and constrictive practices of the Church. Despite the manifest inequalities of society, and a widening gulf between rich and poor, statistically you are more likely to be single and affluent and living alone than at any previous time in history – either because you are separated or divorced, or because you simply have not found or sought a long-term partner. In all likelihood you rent, own, or have thought about owning, a home of your own. You are a product of late-twentieth-century capitalism, increasingly urban in outlook, determined and delineated by consumer choice and consumer demand, and you have available to you the increasingly sophisticated products of the global marketplace. If you have a job, as most Britons do in a country now dominated by service industry (at the time of writing unemployment has dipped, for the first time in 25 years, below 1 million), you are quite likely to be working in front of a computer screen for the best part of the day. There the unlimited capacities of the internet make accessible to you a range of possibilities, in the way of information, consumer goods and networked relationships, so extraordinary and extensive that science fiction has become science fact in the space of just a few years. From 1973, when the first text message was laboriously sent from one Californian computer to another, to the present day, when new technology is fêted as the industrial revolution of our time, so all-encompassing are its effects, we have truly moved into a new age of human activity and potential.

But how brave is this brave new world? Our poor live in Third World conditions; the homeless line our streets; a fifth of our adult population is illiterate; our public services are shoddy and disintegrating; the environment is casually disregarded. And while it is true that many (though certainly not all) people in the UK have more money than previous generations, people are also more anxious, are working longer hours than ever before, are less secure in relationships, and are seemingly as far away from personal happiness as human beings have ever been (according to the *Observer* special supplement, *Britain Uncovered*, nearly 60 per cent of working adults report work stress while 17 per cent of us work more than 48 hours a week). In fact, it is a widely accepted maxim that most people are actually *less* happy than before: that personal fulfilment and feelings of 'groundedness' are chimerical or have a limited life span. In the consumer marketplace, despite the range of goods on offer, the products do not last – they wear out, they get damaged, they are thrown away. Such is the provisionality and brutality of the postmodern condition. The fragility of this land of plenty is well demonstrated by the way personal relationships in the postmodern country so rapidly disintegrate. Glen Duncan writes of just such disintegration in his wonderfully crafted novel *Love Remains*, a coolly analytical autopsy on contemporary love's bitter nihilism. Reflecting on all the failed hopes of her marriage and partnership with Nick, a young woman called Chloë confronts the abyss:

> She couldn't remember what she had imagined this would be like. It hadn't been this. It hadn't been anything. It had been an empty space. He was very far away from her, whoever he was. She could feel language evaporating between them. She wanted to leave.
>
> 'Our life,' he said.
>
> Our life. They had had a life. The day after the wedding. Him making a fire in the hearth. Her making tea, flirting with the role of being a wife, laughing at herself inside, a bit shocked because it titillated her. Twenty-one years old. The other faces from the other life. All the nights of love and sleep; she saw now how much she had believed they would add up to something in the end. Because she hadn't known the end would come before the end, when there was still life left over. (p. 267)

The end often comes before the end adds up to anything at all in life, but the difference between now and former generations is that we no longer know what to do with the sense of waste and of loss. What is left is a feeling of numbness and of absence. A few years ago a striking newspaper photograph was published of three women all facing away from each other but completely engrossed in individual conversations on their mobile phones. The message couldn't be clearer – we all desire some sort of wider connection, but in reality are more separated from one another than ever before. The most chilling metaphor for disconnectedness is the internet, where cyberspace becomes the dominant medium not only for communication but for the activities of the whole of life. The Slovenian cultural theorist Slavoj Žižek discerns two priorities in the equation of community with virtual reality:

> On the one hand there is the dream of the new popularism, in which decentralized networks will allow individuals to band together and to build a grass-roots political system, a transparent world in which the mystery of the impenetrable bureaucratic state agencies is dispelled. On the other, the use of computers and VR to rebuild community results in the

> building of a community inside the machine, reducing individuals to isolated monads, each of them alone, facing a computer, ultimately unsure if the person she or he communicates with on the screen is a 'real' person, a false persona, an agent which combines a number of 'real' people, or a computer program. (*The Plague of Fantasies*, p. 139)

For Žižek, as Graham Ward points out, there is something fetishistic – something atomistic and manufactured – about relationships conducted in cyberspace: they are lacking in meaningful exchange and participation. Hence Multiple User Domains 'become a metaphor for the relay of fantasised erotic relations without real objects', leading to a breakdown of distinction between the real, the imaginary and the symbolic (Ward, p. 149). The blurring of boundaries in cyberspace, between what is and what isn't real, as well as what is and isn't acceptable, together with the atomised and individualistic nature of the use of VR, is a disturbing indicator of why pornography on the net is both so ubiquitous and so popular. This cannot but affect adversely the development of healthy relationships between individuals which are not subject to computer control, and which are dependent rather on face-to-face encounter and the vicissitudes of chance. But as society becomes more and more individualised, and oriented towards self-encounter rather than towards genuine notions of community, it becomes much more difficult for individuals to engage with another person or prospective partner in a spirit of reciprocal self-giving. We must not altogether demonise the web, or fall into the Luddite trap of dismissing new technology as inherently harmful. After all, there is much good that access to the internet can bring, especially in the beneficial exchange of information, or in the process of giving people access to educational aids on a much more effective scale than ever before. Nevertheless, there is a danger too that in the ubiquity of computer and internet use, we will lose sight of what meaningful relationships consist of, and how these should be conducted, when they are neither limited to the confines of our PC screens, nor manufactured by them.

One of the most effective recent treatments of the ambiguous world of virtual reality is to be found in Christopher Priest's disturbing novel *The Extremes*, where a woman – and former FBI agent – called Teresa repeatedly enters a virtual reality world known as Extreme Experience in order to come to terms with her husband's death at the hands of a gunman. Exposure to ExEx leads to the stripping away of all her – and our – certainties about the nature of reality, time and context, so that Teresa's highly ambiguous rehabilitation is to be found in the end only through her total withdrawal into the world she herself has manufactured. However, the disorienting dislocations between this world and the 'real world' she has left behind are so expertly done by Priest that we, the readers, begin to wonder whether there is any distinction between the two worlds in a 'true' or meaningful sense at all. Virtual reality becomes as tangible and solid as the real, so that 'reality' itself continually invites deconstruction and redefinition. This parable sounds far-fetched, but it truthfully encapsulates the prevalent sense of disharmony and disorientation that chips away at all our realities at the start of the third millennium. And it is mirrored by the same author's earlier work, especially *The Glamour*, where the inter-relationship between identity, memory and madness is explored just as powerfully and discordantly. Similar themes are explored elsewhere in popular culture, notably in the cyberpunk films *Johnny Mnemonic* (1995), *eXistenZ* (1999) and *The Matrix* (1999), and most recently in Christopher Nolan's brilliantly conceived movie *Memento* (2000). Here the main protagonist, portrayed by Guy Pearce, attempts in vain to piece together a life from memories (are they genuine or manufactured?) which evaporate within minutes, opening him up to fatal manipulation by third parties. In this instance form and content are perfectly matched, since the film teases and beguiles its viewers by mazily unwinding backwards, beginning at the end of the story and concluding at the beginning – in its twists, turns and dense complexities, the ultimate postmodern deception. In Chapter 6 I shall look in more detail at the way the postmodern is explored through film.

If the internet becomes the dominant metaphor as well as the fundamental communicative mode of postmodernity, what of postmodernity itself? People often talk about the condition of postmodernity, but it is by no means clear that they all mean the same thing, or whether one can generalise about it in any very helpful sense at all. One of the best accounts of postmodernity and postmodernism is to be found in Gerard Loughlin's book *Telling God's Story*:

> Postmodernism is the idea that the once hoped-for future of the human race has arrived. It is not a new age because all ages have come to an end, and now everything that once was is to be recuperated and used – as we like – in our fashioning. There is a vast proliferation in all areas of life, but without direction, for without a future there can be no direction or point to our endeavours. We are not governed but managed, and efficiency is our watchword. But we no longer know why or care. For some this is wonderful; for others it is more terrible than anything imagined by the Seer of Patmos. (p. 5)

In this account we see some of the recurring themes preoccupying those who write about the postmodern. It is a condition assuming various forms (which might be architectural, philosophical or sociological) without any abiding governing principle, evincing endless random growth, whose various components can be used and re-used as we see fit, but whose manifestations appear ultimately as futile in themselves and therefore as eminently disposable or recyclable. Postmodernism, therefore, is a 'fashioning of commodities – of films, food and clothes, and of people (who no longer have characters but life-styles)' (*Telling God's Story*, pp. 5–6). Loughlin usefully distinguishes between modernism – where the idea is that humanity is the maker of its own destiny, upwardly mobile in pursuit of social and technological advancement – and postmodernism (which has supplanted it), where the utopianism of the future has been replaced by the idea that the grand narratives of the past have lost all credibility, that idealism looks naïve, and that 'there are no master stories left' (ibid., p. 9). Although in many ways complex and contradictory, modernism is fundamentally an *optimistic* phenomenon. Employing rational modes of social organisation and of thought – such rationality deriving from the thinking of the Enlightenment – it pursues human emancipation from superstition and mystification. But as David Harvey makes clear, in his book *The Condition of Postmodernity,* 'The twentieth century – with its death camps and death squads, its militarism and two world wars, its threat of nuclear annihilation and its experience of Hiroshima and Nagasaki – has certainly shattered this optimism' (p. 13). The notion that there might be a single corpus of 'truth' to which everybody has access, or a homogeneity of human aspiration, looks absurd according to this picture. Relativism and reductionism rule the day. Truth is a redundant idea, monolithic – and now post-demolition – rubble. There are many perspectives, all equally valid, all deserving of consideration, and everything is possible. This is a different kind of liberation, and in its celebratory embrace of the ephemeral and the fissiparous, 'postmodernism swims, even wallows in the fragmentary and chaotic currents of change as if that is all there is' (p. 44). The consequences of this existential deregulation are as follows:

> Here we are as postmoderns! We are our own little storytellers, living among the ruins of our former grand narratives. We tell stories purely for pleasure. Today we tell one story and tomorrow we will tell another. Stories are fashionable; we change them with the seasons, as we change our clothes. Perhaps because this is a new game, we make our stories out of the rubble of the old narratives we find lying around. We mix and match, liking the fun of spotting where the bits have come from. Our novels and films are full of quotes and allusions; our buildings are a little classical, a little rococo, a little gothic, and even, sometimes, a little modernist. Our values and morals are equally various, equally changeable, commodities like everything else. (p. 9)

As Loughlin has observed, many have indeed found postmodernity a liberating phenomenon, especially when, hand in hand with secularisation, the dominance of the old certainties has been pushed back. This process has allowed people to think more adventurously and creatively in their lives, to explore different avenues, and to interact with one another in ways that would not necessarily have been condoned thirty years ago. The absence of master or meta-narratives means that there is so much more in the way of personal choice than ever before. No longer is it mandatory for people to get married before living together. No longer is it necessary to conform by getting married in church. No longer is it even particularly shocking, at least to the ears I think of most people in Britain, to announce that one's sexual partner is of the same gender as oneself, or has a different coloured skin. People have been encouraged to take personal responsibility for their lives and behaviour, and for what they may achieve in society, and to challenge orthodoxies which are redundant, or close to being so. The established Church, the royal family, and Parliament at Westminster are all institutions which have lately been challenged to provide interrogative self-justification, and rightly so. Much of this should be welcomed, especially when in social and political terms it has meant the liberation of women to a much greater degree, the legalisation of homosexuality, improved race relations, and a more open and tolerant society in general.

In some ways, of course, greater capacity for choice has not necessarily meant more liberalisation or openness or – as the dance anthem by D:Ream has it – that 'things can only get better': the various Conservative governments of the eighties and early nineties demonstrated that all too forcefully. And in several areas, especially with regard to racial equality, health, crime, education, and accessibility of opportunity for the impoverished, there is still considerable room for improvement, as New Labour at the time of writing is having openly to admit, and as recent ethnic rioting in England's mill towns depressingly underlines. However, despite increased room for personal development (which – in its religious manifestations – I will explore in the next chapter), it remains the case that adherence in society to the culture of late capitalism, with the rapacious consumerism that goes with it, has led to a greater sense of *fin de siècle*; of the loss of some essential definition to our lives. At one time Christianity was able to provide this, or at least the indicators of which road to travel. No longer. Weakened, marginalised, and sidetracked into self-important and sometimes ridiculed proclamations (who on the street recalls George Carey's much-trumpeted Decade of Evangelism, or even knows when it was?), the Church of England is unable to lend any effective support to Žižek's plea for moderation in what we buy and sell, and how we conduct ourselves:

> Instead of stable products destined to last for generations, capitalism introduces a breathtaking dynamics of obsolescence. We are bombarded by new or newer products which are sometimes obsolete even before they come fully into use – PCs have to be replaced every year if one is to keep up with the Joneses, long-playing records were replaced by CDs, and now by DVDs. The aftermath of this constant innovation is, of course, the permanent production of piles of discarded waste. (*The Fragile Absolute*, p. 40)

What seems to me to be missing, to a greater and greater degree, is a sense within people of the importance of mystery in their lives, of the significance of developing an inner spiritual life, and the necessity of challenging the hegemony of consumption. Unhindered by any significant counter-current towards compassion, community and the common good, the capitalist drive pushes us further towards self-gratification, where the uppermost objective becomes the acquisition of more 'stuff'. This might either take the form simply of the accumulation of more possessions, or it might mean a search for distraction in finding new 'things', such as the sights and sounds of unfamiliar places through travel. In both cases, however, the drive is towards disengagement from responsibility, from other people, both corporately and individually, but ultimately also from knowledge of oneself. One consequence of this imperative is that those who for whatever reason are unable to acquire this 'stuff' are pushed out towards the margins, crushed by an implacable economy of credit and debt. Other consequences are more insidious. In her brilliant and parabolic novel *Where Are the Snows*, Maggie Gee offers keen insights into what happens to a wealthy middle-aged couple, Christopher and Alexandra, who decide to leave their house, children and former lives behind, and embark on an odyssey of travel, unencumbered by what they see as the dull baggage of convention. In the end, what starts as an adventure and the mad gaiety of escape consumes both characters. They are confronted with the emptiness of what they have done and the consequences of what they have left behind: children who regard them with antipathy, a relationship with each other that has soured through betrayal and selfishness, and only death to look forward to:

> Together we travelled all over the world, a glittering, shifting mosaic of places. Odd how few end up meaning anything. And so I come back again and again to the same ones, because they have meaning. Not because they are exotic, or strange. Because I loved them . . . Looking back now from twenty years later I realise I loved the house in Islington, even though I went round the world to escape it . . . And now, in my mind, I come back to them all, the well-known places, and there aren't so many, for now I can't escape any more, now I have to find somewhere to die. (p. 356)

Alexandra, wracked in the end by cancer and chemotherapy, is compelled to take stock of her life, and what she discovers is that she is part of a network of complex relationships and responsibilities that make final evasion impossible: she wants to be part of something that she has spent much of her life trying to leave. And now, at the moment of true departure, she looks forward to death as a kind of homecoming:

> It's all a matter of time, and perception. Christopher never leaves me now. We left the children and we left each other; we abandoned the world, and the snows melted. We used the world until it grew tired. Now I want to be given back to it. (p. 376)

This kind of orientation towards individualism, at all sorts of social levels, is a blight on our age; it is a condition that excludes others and feeds on itself, resulting in a self-obsessed interiority.

For example, the contestants in the second series of the popular Channel 4 'docusoap' *Big Brother* referred not once to the forthcoming general election of June 2001, despite the fact that it had dominated news headlines for weeks. They were much too preoccupied with their own body image and the prospect of fame to be bothered by culture or politics. In itself this might seem a trivial thing. But when, on a larger scale, self-oriented tribalism, unlimited technological development and rampant capitalism are mixed together there is every indication that the lack of room for theological wisdom will be disastrous. As Peter Selby puts it, 'we have arrived at a point where the world and national economies cannot be declared just, let alone Christian, in their outworking' (*Grace and Mortgage*, p. 161). A case in point might be George Bush's rejection of the Kyoto Protocol on climate control because the treaty is allegedly contrary to the United States' 'national' (read economic) 'interests'. Appalling as it is, such naked self-regard (the US produces one quarter of all harmful global emissions), accompanied by flagrant disdain both for the clear scientific evidence of global warming and the consensus of opinion among the international community, is in one sense merely a sign of the times. Obsession with 'national' self-interest, furthermore, may become even more destructive in the cause of overt nationalism or ethnic domination, as the many recent Balkan conflicts have so terribly reminded us. Affluence, urbanisation and the misuse of technology in one part of the world increasingly spell poverty, drought, malnutrition and war in another. The paradox of 'globalisation' is that it allows for little sense of global community, except as understood in the most basic sense of the exchange of capital or goods or commodities from one part of the world to another. And this is far from being a fair and regulated process, since the odds are stacked against the losers: the rich get richer and the poor poorer. Even in the urban first world, 'progress' can at best be viewed ambiguously. The social theorist Mike Davis indicates as much in his influential book *City of Quartz*, which reveals a perilously schizophrenic and dystopian Los Angeles ('a stand-in for capitalism in general', p. 18):

> Welcome to post-liberal Los Angeles, where the defence of luxury lifestyles is translated into a proliferation of new repressions in space and movement, undergirded by the ubiquitous 'armed response'. This obsession with physical security systems, and, collaterally, with the architectural policing of social boundaries, has become a zeitgeist of urban restructuring, a master narrative in the emerging built environment of the 1990s. Yet contemporary urban theory, whether debating the role of electronic technologies in precipitating 'postmodern space', or discussing the dispersion of urban functions across poly-centred metropolitan 'galaxies', has been strangely silent about the militarization of city life so grimly visible at the street level. Hollywood's pop apocalypses and pulp science fiction have been more realistic, and politically perceptive, in representing the programmed hardening of the urban surface in the wake of the social polarizations of the Reagan era. Images of carceral inner-cities (*Escape from New York*, *Running Man*), high-tech police death squads (*Blade Runner*), sentient buildings (*Die Hard*), urban Bantustans (*They Live!*), Vietnam-like street wars (*Colors*), and so on, only extrapolate from already existing trends. (p. 223)

Davis might have gone on to mention, except that it appeared just after his book was published, Joel Schumacher's much admired film *Falling Down* (1992). In this movie Michael Douglas plays a man pushed to the edge and beyond by LA's crumbling socio-political infrastructure. He decides to 'strike back' on behalf of the common man by taking out his frustration on several of the city's less salubrious inhabitants in a picaresque attempt to walk home, having first abandoned his car in the midst of one of the seemingly endless jams that characterise the urban freeways. Despite attracting criticism for some of its racist overtones (a number of the assailants Douglas encounters and resists are Hispanic, and he is white), the film is widely perceived as a powerful encapsulation of the contemporary urban postmodern condition. There are malignant forces at work in the world; there is little adequate or concerted response to them from the authorities; therefore one must resist them individually. Any notion of an inherent common good is sheer sentiment; every man is an island, and he must protect it and himself accordingly. The result is that 'In cities like Los Angeles, on the bad edge of postmodernity, one observes an unprecedented tendency to merge urban design, architecture and the police apparatus into a single, comprehensive security effort' (Davis, p. 224).

Insecurity, depression, breakdown, rage, emptiness: these are the sinister handmaidens of postmodernity. Hand in hand with the breakdown experienced by individuals is the breakdown of corporate trust between groups, communities and countries, resulting in suspicion, mistreatment and conflict. So-called special interest groups abound in Britain, and one can be sure that in most instances the one thing that they will all have in common is their mutual hostility (consider the divisions detected recently between what is often portrayed – if caricatured – as a superior and uncaring urban governing elite and a misunderstood, neglected rural community with its backs to the wall). Loss of a sense of community is everywhere, and the Church and much theology has little effective to say about it. In order to get to grips with a reality that most people can recognise, theology needs credibly to engage with the less wholesome side of life: with its pain, its disappointments and its dreads, with the reflections of what Stephen Pattison has elsewhere called 'The Shadow Side of Jesus'. As Pattison says, theology, like the founder of Christianity, 'may need to lose its life to gain it' ('Public Theology: A Polemical Epilogue', *Political Theology*, p. 74). It must be prepared 'to disappear into the world to merge with crowds of discourses and people who may occasionally be helped by the wisdom and insights of some of its contributions' (ibid.). This means acknowledging first that the Church has failed to make an impact on upcoming generations, and facing that fact bravely and openly. It has lost the generation aged 17 to 35. Second, it means admitting that theology needs to find fresh resources in order to convey the important truths to which it certainly has access, and without which much of importance is lost. I shall turn to these resources later on. In the meantime, we can be sure that what this does not mean is a continuation of the kind of theology that talks only about joy or happiness or the universal efficacy of endurance. Tell that to the single mother on the estate, left by her partner, who scratches a living on a paucity of benefits. Or the desperate student who sees no light at the end of the tunnel other than his nightly phone call to the Samaritans. Or the middle-aged man made prematurely redundant without resource to the skills necessary to find further work. Or those who exist in the world without love from a partner, or the support of friends. Nevertheless, it remains the case that, despite all of this fragmentation and suffering, the ugliness of the world is often considered to be mitigated – though not redeemed – by its beauty; and the imperative to look towards beauty and truth is one of the perennial characteristics of human beings. Consider Milan Kundera:

> She said to herself when once the onslaught of ugliness became completely unbearable, she would go to a florist and buy a forget-me-not, a slender stalk with miniature blue flowers. She would go out into the street holding the flower before her eyes, staring at it tenaciously so as to see only that single beautiful blue point, to see it as the last thing she wanted to preserve for herself from a world she had ceased to love. (*Immortality*, p. 22)

We need new resources for a world that in so many respects has become unlovable. Our postmodern world, with all its glittering opportunities, its freedoms of choice, its openings, can so easily become a prison if it lacks love or understanding or wisdom. It is the drive towards these, and the vacuum traditional theological teaching has left behind, that have prompted many people in our society to look elsewhere for the weapons with which they may fight the cynicism and selfishness of secular capitalism – as well as find themselves in the process. In the end, what everybody is looking for is happiness, and wherever that is to be found is not necessarily to be denigrated, whatever Church teaching may have to say on the matter. Of course some resources are more authentic than others, and I shall attempt to define some ways of differentiating between valid and invalid repositories of theological wisdom in the next chapter. Later on I shall discuss some of the films of the late Soviet director Andrei Tarkovsky, in an attempt to show how one man approached the task of restoring reverence and harmony to a deterministic and rationalistic world which he regarded as rushing, in its self-absorption and materialism, headlong towards self-destruction. Thereby we will see how his work may help us in our own quest for authentic spiritual resources. For the moment, however, I wish to draw attention to the book that inspired *Stalker,* one of his greatest films, and which itself represents one of the most prophetic responses to the condition of postmodernity as well as a suggested antidote to some of its excesses.

*Roadside Picnic* by the Strugatsky brothers envisages a world some time in the near future which has been subject to visitations from space. These visitors have left behind them several 'zones' within which certain objects may be found that defy the laws of human physics. These artefacts, this celestial debris, are the rubbish left behind by the aliens' 'picnic'. So valuable are the objects in the zones that they are sold on for vast sums, often on the black market. However, the zones themselves are now so dangerous, and subject to such violent and unpredictable paranormal events, that only hardened criminal 'stalkers' have the expertise and knowledge to retrieve the desired booty without ill-consequence. Even then, the stalkers (and their families) themselves suffer mysterious ailments and disfigurements as a result of their activities. In the book's denouement, a stalker called Redrick Schuhart determines to visit the zone in which he operates one final time, after several perilous trips, in order to bring back a fabled object called the Golden Ball. This reputedly grants wishes to those who ask of it. Red's determination to succeed, despite the many dangers involved, is explained by his daughter's genetic disfigurement because of his illegal profession. He wishes to bring back the Ball to heal Monkey (so-called because of the silky fur that entirely covers her body), and is prepared to sacrifice his companion in the Zone, Arthur, the son of a rival stalker, to gain his objective. In an extraordinary concluding passage, Red is seen clambering over the ravaged industrial waste of the Zone towards his goal.

But so tormented is he by the final words of the dead Arthur, whose mangled corpse lies behind him, that he is unable to remember his own wish: he can only reiterate the ardent longings expressed by the lost boy. In its depiction of a capricious world comprised of bits and pieces of dangerous 'stuff', a sort of *bricolage* whose purpose is at once desirable and unfathomable – the waste product of a futuristic race – and in its highly ambiguous ending, where individual satisfaction is supplanted by an appeal to the redemption of all humankind, mediated through sacrifice, *Roadside Picnic* poses one of the most uncomfortable and powerful theological challenges to the postmodern condition that I know:

> The sun was broiling hot, red spots floated before his eyes, the air was quivering on the floor of the quarry, and in the shimmer it seemed that the ball was dancing in place like a buoy on the waves. He went past the bucket, superstitiously picking up his feet higher and making sure not to step on the splotches. And then, sinking into the rubble, he dragged himself across the quarry to the dancing, winking ball. He was covered with sweat and panting from the heat, and at the same time a chill was running through him, he was shuddering, as if he had a bad hangover, and the sweet chalk dust gritted between his teeth. He had stopped trying to think. He just repeated his litany over and over: 'I am an animal, you see that. I don't have the words, they didn't teach me the words. I don't know how to think, the bastards didn't let me learn how to think. But if you really are . . . all-powerful . . . all-knowing . . . then you figure it out! Look into my heart. I know that everything you need is there. It has to be. I never sold my soul to anyone! It's mine, it's human! You take from me what it is I want . . . It just can't be that I would want something bad! Damn it all, I can't think of anything, except those words of his . . . "HAPPINESS FOR EVERYBODY, FREE, AND NO ONE WILL GO AWAY UNSATISFIED!" ' (p. 145)

In this context death might be explicable, as John Bowker puts it, as 'opportunity as well as end' (*The Meanings of Death*, p. 220).

Arthur's sacrifice, shocking as it is, makes it possible for Red to relinquish his own particular needs in such a way that he re-establishes connection with a wider humanity. Paradoxically, the alien world of the Zone has enabled him to move away from atomism towards a new recognition of the human community of which he is – despite having existed on the margins of society – intrinsically part. Furthermore, having been fundamentally self-interested throughout the whole story, Red is now able to look beyond himself to something or someone other than him and his own immediate family, and articulate a transcendent sensibility oriented towards the common good. The motifs of sacrificial death, transcendence, and charitable compassion will be familiar to many of those who call themselves Christians.

# CHAPTER 3

# Alternative Spiritualities and Theologies

It seems to be mandatory among Christians to write off the burgeoning spiritualities and holistic beliefs and practices of the New Age movement as nonsense. Most of this hostility comes down to the following factors: that the New Age is a farrago of disconnected and self-indulgent 'feelings' about human beings and the universe that have little or no basis in 'truth'; that it has little wider moral or ethical concern, being oriented pretty much exclusively towards the self; that it lacks self-discipline; that it lacks valid textual and historical authority; and that it is, generally speaking, anti-communitarian, being primarily preoccupied with individualistic self-development and self-improvement. Part of the difficulty inherent in this critique, of course, is that the 'New Age' is by no means a homogeneous movement or collection of doctrines about which generalisations can easily be made. As William Bloom, editor of a recent collection of New Age texts, points out:

> The very nature of the postmodern global village – the contemporary way of researching, perceiving and interpreting – is that people do and will seek information as widely as possible. It is absolutely logical, then, that religion and religious inquiry will also begin to reflect these new circumstances. It will tend to be international, universalist, process-oriented, pluralistic, diverse, democratic, networked

> and decentralized. Reflecting the free-flowing accessibility of information, the new religious approach will also tend to be an open information system and not one of closed beliefs. All of this is exactly the nature of the holistic approach. (*Holistic Revolution*, p. xiii)

Its pluralistic, heterogeneous nature makes it difficult, therefore, to define precisely what 'New Age' doctrine amounts to, except that – and this is certainly how Bloom sees it – it is complementary to existing religious and belief systems in its promotion of universality. Accordingly, the holistic movement is actively engaged with all spiritual traditions, whatever they may be or say:

> It embraces them and is interested in how similar they are and how they complement each other. Here, in fact, is a clear example of how the holistic supermarket and post-modern relativism can work to everyone's benefit. The Ten Commandments are not in competition with the Sermon on the Mount or the Buddha's Eightfold Path or any of the injunctions from other faiths. They are all respected and drawn upon. They reinforce each other. (p. xvi)

There is a paradoxical nature to this welcoming and inclusivist side of New Age belief, however, since Bloom also recognises that it is precisely in its inclusivism where the main challenge to religious orthodoxy is to be found. Since all monopolies on truth are questioned and overthrown, there can be no single perspective on how, why and wherefore we are as we are and we worship as we do:

> We are in changing times and today, for many people, religious certainty does not seem such an attractive option. This is not just a matter of aesthetics. Anyone with the slightest knowledge of psychology or emotional intelligence recognizes that people with a fundamentalist certainty about their ideas – those who are not open to listening to and respecting other viewpoints – are either ignorant or insecure.

> Rigid conviction is no longer seen as an admirable role model for leadership. A monolithic belief system seems primitive and oppressive. It is a cultural dinosaur. (p. xv)

We begin to have a sense, then, of what this holistic or New Age spiritual–religious phenomenon might amount to: a plethora of perspectives on the nature of reality and human being which is open-ended and open-minded, but at the same time strongly critical of 'fundamentalism'. This is equated not necessarily with what Christians or Muslims might ordinarily understand as 'fundamentalist' – adopting an extreme position on certain beliefs and practices that run against the main religious grain – but as *any* ideological stand on beliefs and practices which excludes diversity or multifaceted spiritual freedom of expression.

Such an outlook is absolutely consistent with the general post-modern turn, where monolithic systems of all kinds are torn down, where established Christianity is perceived to be authoritarian and anachronistic, as well as unfashionable, and where there are much more attractive wares on offer elsewhere. After all, why buy one brand of baked beans in the Co-op when you can get hold of ten different brands in Waitrose (not to mention those other goods which until lately could only be purchased in a posh delicatessen)? This hypermarket approach to religion and spirituality is strongly defended by Bloom as being appealingly democratic and non-hierarchical ('people should be free to explore meaning and reality in as many ways as are available', he states [p. xiii]). In some respects he is absolutely right to make a stand against a restrictive approach to spirituality which is out of keeping both with the *zeitgeist*, and with the pace of people's aspirations and innermost needs. On the debit side, he is also, like many supporters and practitioners of the New Age, wrong to suppose that just because 'anything goes' it is necessarily also valuable. One might as well argue that all kinds of political activity, regardless of their ideological standpoints, are as interesting and usefully pedagogical as each other. The lessons of history have their own tale to tell. And it is in its detachment from historical, post-Holocaust outcomes, that holistic doctrine is perhaps most vulnerable to critique.

Despite its openness, its cross-cultural and multi-disciplinary attractiveness, which exactly matches the liberalisation and democratisation of society at large, the holistic movement often lacks self-control or self-regulation. It also suffers from the burden of self-justification, unlike Christianity, which – despite its present weakness – has nevertheless survived over two millennia. In some ways this doesn't seem to matter very much. After all, why worry if somebody is engaged in crystal ball gazing or reading the runes if these activities have little adverse social or political impact on anybody else? Of course, such practices may be psychologically harmful just to those individuals who adhere to them if they foster a perspective on life which is all-encompassing yet manifestly nonsensical and ultimately misconstrued. But there is a wider danger that all sorts of other activities, which demonstrably *are* group- or movement-based, are legitimised by the holistic broad brush even where these are maleficent, aggressively subversive or socially corrosive. That is where theology at its best seems to me to have something important to say in defence of traditional doctrine and metaphysics. In a historically resonant faith-tradition (tested and found wanting by Dachau and Auschwitz) there is invariably a sense of how theological deregulation can be harnessed, consciously or unconsciously, to the worst of social and political ends. The quisling German Christian Movement – to which Dietrich Bonhoeffer was tenaciously antagonistic – demonstrated this all too forcefully. Similarly, for Jürgen Moltmann, theology must now speak from 'behind barbed wire', as it were: 'The criticism of the church and theology which we have been fortunate enough to experience, and which is justified on sociological, psychological and ideological grounds, can only be accepted and made radical by a *critical* theology of the cross' (*The Crucified God*, p. 2, emphasis mine).

Despite these concerns, it needs to be admitted by theologians that large numbers of people find in New Age doctrines much of what they do not find in Christianity; and the numbers of adherents to holistic practices and beliefs are growing (Bloom, p. xi). Just how difficult it is to homogenise these activities is emphasised by Tanya Luhrmann, the author of a seminal late-eighties study of modern British witchcraft. The New Age, she writes, is:

> . . . a broad cultural ideology, a development of the countercultural sixties, which privileges holistic medicine, 'intuitive sciences' like astrology and tarot, ecological and anti-nuclear political issues, and alternative therapies, medicines and philosophers. The 'New Age' has become a widely-accepted catch-phrase for this matrix of concerns: there are 'New Age' medicines, music, meditation tapes, and 'New Age' centres which offer classes in herbalism and Akido. Another name for this set of interests and attitudes is 'Aquarian'. Talk about the 'New Age' or Aquarian Age is utopian and idealistic: when it arrives people will work together, there will be neither hierarchy nor loss of individuality, and science will be used for constructive purposes only. (*Persuasions of the Witch's Craft*, p. 30)

The publishers of William Bloom's collection claim in their cover publicity that the book is unrivalled in its range and scope, which – in terms just of printed matter – may well be true. However, one has only to begin browsing the internet to see that even *Holistic Revolution*, weighing in at well over 400 pages, is but the tip of the holistic iceberg, given the enormity of New Age choice that is on offer. The internet bookseller Amazon.co.uk lists ten categories of reading under its 'Mind, Body, Spirit' section, each of which subdivides into numerous other – sometimes overlapping – sections and topics. The resulting range of choice is quite staggering, and goes well beyond Bloom's – ironically enough – relatively conservative-looking chapter-headings of 'New Science', 'Psychology', 'Gaia', 'Holistic Health', 'Feminism and the Goddess', 'Shamanic and Magical Traditions', 'Mystic and Esoteric Religion', and 'Modern Prophecy'. The ten basic Amazon categories are as follows: complementary medicine; divination; earth-based religion; mythology; occultism; paranormal and unexplained phenomena; self-help; spirituality; thought and practice; and other religious and spiritual practices. So far so good. But from these derive a whole universe of possible paths to follow: astrology, cartomancy, clairvoyance and precognition, crystals, fortune telling, graphology, numerology, palmistry, phrenology, prophecy, runes, tarot; aliens, crop circles, ghosts and poltergeists, the paranormal, spirit communication, the supernatural, UFOs, unexplained mysteries; Druids, Gaia, Native American beliefs, Shamanism, witchcraft and Wicca; acupuncture, acupressure, aromatherapy, Ayurveda, chiropractic/ osteopathy, healing, herbal remedies, holism, homeopathy, naturopathy, reflexology, massage; Feng Shui, meditation, ESP, dreams, auras and colours, astral projection, chakras, mental and spiritual healing, metaphysical phenomena, reincarnation, spiritualism, theosophy, and Urantia – and so on.

Self-evidently it would be possible to write a whole book – or even several books – just on these subjects by themselves. So how is it possible, given the pluriform and intangible nature of what, clearly by convenience, we designate 'New Age belief', to distinguish any defining characteristics? Holistic beliefs and practices clearly *are* manifestations of the reaction against exclusivist belief systems or ideological positions, and as such are absolutely consonant with the characteristics of secular postmodernity. In that respect, therefore, we can view holistic beliefs and practices merely as popular expressions of people's innermost wants and needs, this time with a spiritual as distinct from a secular bent. They (or at least the better-established ones) appear to offer people both a lifestyle choice and a sense of belonging to a community of like-minded individuals. Furthermore, they have a clearly signalled commitment to developing notions of individualisation and identity, and this is something which Christianity is often perceived to do less well. In the important sense, then, that alternative spiritualities provide people with a sense of 'groundedness' and the possibility of self-knowledge, they already have their own kind of authenticity, and resist easy dismissal.

The death of Diana, Princess of Wales, in August 1997 showcased, in a very concentrated form, all of these various components, enabling a great many different sections of society to empathise absolutely with what Diana had come to represent, and, in a quasi-religious manner, to respond accordingly. Anthony Holden writes:

> The extraordinary scenes in the week of her funeral, when grown men belied the supposed national character by weeping in the streets, and strangers by hugging each other, weren't the half of it. Drawn to join the mutinous crowds, advancing menacingly on Buckingham Palace, was a host of disenfranchised refugees from Britain's neglected minorities, who would never have attended any royal occasion *per se*, but saw in Diana a figure who had somehow represented their interests in high places. ('What was Di For?', *Observer Review*)

The significance of Diana, for this writer, is that she came to be seen by people from all walks of life to have incarnated in her own person some powerful metaphysical truth, and thus had metamorphosed from a shy teenager into 'that rare breed of universal figure by whom we are all enabled to read ourselves' (ibid.). But this was no fairy-tale ending of continuing adoration for the martyr. In an age where everything, even people, have become just so many disposable commodities, the princess was barely cold in her coffin before the nation got back to business as usual:

> In death, she surpassed even her own potent standards of symbolism, leaving behind a tantalising vision of what might have been, as Britain so soon forgot her, wondered what all the fuss had been about, and slumped back into its familiar want of self-belief, not to mention, in the case of the English, an acute identity crisis. (Holden, ibid.)

Any attempt to differentiate between aspects of the New Age immediately shows that it is truly kaleidoscopic in the variety of patterns it offers. However, this being the age of the post-modern, and the context of global capitalism, much of the popular interest in holistic matters has been harnessed to thoroughly commercial and selfish ends, thereby neutralising the very spirit of anti-materialism that informs the movement more generally. I am thinking here of the somewhat notorious 'self-help' industry, a voracious marketplace for generalised notions of self-betterment, articulated in a frenzy of advertising, newspapers, magazines and popular journals, and mediated via expressions of pop psychology and simplified, westernised versions of eastern philosophical thought-systems such as Feng Shui.

It is notable how thoroughly materialistic so much of modern Feng Shui is in its concerns. At least one representative manual about putting its ideas into practice (like the majority of the numerous books in this area, this looks more like a catalogue for Habitat or IKEA than a practical handbook) is subtitled *Your Practical Guide to Health, Wealth and Happiness* (Simon Brown, *Essential Feng Shui*). It thus unashamedly equates well-being with acquisitiveness. Correspondingly, many newspapers and magazines nowadays (predominantly women's magazines, but increasingly publications targeting the expanding market for men's lifestyle and 'men's health') have regular articles on positive self-development. There is little preoccupation here with anything other than what are essentially ways of feeling better about oneself or of making one's immediate environment more attractive, frequently through the purchase of various kinds of goods. Legitimate or illegitimate as those objectives may be, they are not grounded in much more than the self-absorption so characteristic of the secular condition, and seem to have little application to the wider community. Neither is there any sense of serious cosmological interest. The entire focus is on the self. The present-day cult of youth, of wanting to make oneself look younger, which can just as easily be interpreted as a denial of mortality and degeneration, is another less attractive aspect of the movement as a whole. When certain holistic therapies are marketed using the most aggressive techniques, this directly mirrors identical secular anxieties.

Nevertheless, to counterbalance these materialistic tendencies are much more interesting holistic manifestations. In such movements as Gaia, and in the followers of earth-based spiritualities like Druidry, shamanism and modern witchcraft (or Wicca), can be discerned a genuine reverence for creation which encompasses all of life and celebrates the deep-rooted folk and spiritual traditions of this country's ancestors. Practitioners of these 'pagan' movements are often derided or mistrusted, especially by Christians, but according to Bloom their chief concern is nothing more or less than the environment and its sacred dimensions: 'They have a direct and unselfconscious personal experience of the beauty and spirit of nature and of the universe. It is reasonable to imagine a time when all hunter-gathering and early pastoral peoples had this natural religious experience' (p. xvii). For every couple of MBS books entitled something like *You Can Heal Your Life* or *How to Get What You Really Want* there are several others which are seriously engaged with the damaging consequences of human beings' disconnection from the notions that all of life is interdependent, and that our misuse of the planet's resources threatens us with extinction. These ideas are thoroughly bound up with a reclamation of reverence for the spiritualities that are immanent in the earth itself, with a view to articulating a holistic spirituality of all creation. Much of this is laudable. In its thoroughgoing concern for community it goes way beyond mainstream Christian theology, which by and large has been little concerned with responsible ecological custodianship, having been too much influenced by the appropriative and utilitarian theology of the Book of Genesis (see Genesis 1:28–30).

Such eco-spiritual traditions (they owe much to J. E. Lovelock's fundamental idea, in his book *Gaia: A New Look at Life on Earth*, that the earth functions as a single organism) have considerable appeal to a wide swathe of people who are attracted to an umbrella assemblage of green, anti-capitalist, anti-globalist ideas, and who react against the determinant materialism, wasteful consumerism and individualised selfishness of the day. The links between certain holistic ideas and the anti-capitalist demonstrations in London of May Day 2000, for instance, are indicated not least by the fact that the organisers of the protests used as one of their chief points of contact a bookshop in east Oxford specialising in New Age spirituality. In their contempt for the establishment and their hatred of globalisation and big corporations, these followers of New Age ideas epitomise a more general disaffection with old models for religion and society, which they see as repressive, redundantly monolithic and favouring the few at the expense of the many. Yet it is notable how, despite rejecting the outward forms of doctrinal orthodoxy, and the social structures which go with them, exponents of alternative spiritualities often end up rejuvenating ideas and beliefs which would by no means be out of place in a reformed version of Christianity. One can see this clearly in the case of the Burning Man festival, an event held every Labor Day weekend in the Black Rock Desert, Nevada.

Burning Man originated when its founder Larry Harvey burned an effigy of a human figure, for his own personal feelings of catharsis, on a San Francisco beach in 1986. Since then, a festival of Glastonbury-sized proportions has grown up around a weekend of performance art in the baking Nevada sun, to which thousands of revellers, predominantly from the Bay area – but increasingly from all over the world – are drawn. Matt Wray sets the scene in his article on the festival, 'Burning Man':

> There are all sorts here, a living breathing encyclopedia of subcultures; desert survivalists, urban primitives, artists, rocketeers, hippies, deadheads, queers, pyromaniacs, cybernauts, musicians, ranters, eco-freaks, acidheads, breeders, punks, gun-lovers, dancers, S/M and bondage enthusiasts, nudists, refugees from the men's movement, anarchists, ravers, transgender types and New Age spiritualists. In the course of the weekend, participants will, among other things, set up FM radio stations, print a daily newspaper, build a desert rave camp, and soak in the muddy heat of surrounding hot springs. All this activity takes place as a way of expressing our desire for collective action, collective experience in the face of all that threatens to keep us isolated from one another. We've come to form a small town, an intentional but impermanent community. We've come here to burn the Man. ('Burning Man', *Bad Subjects*)

The festivities culminate when the effigy is set on fire and destroyed by the revellers, leading to a rocket-fuelled frenzy of dance and celebration as all the negativities and disappointments of the past year are ritually expurgated:

> Outlined and rigged in blue neon, the Man glows ghostly at night, powerful generators humming at its feet. He stands ready to be destroyed. On Sunday night, the final evening of the event, there is a black tie cocktail party, followed by a festive parade procession out to the Man. Then at the height of the pre-burn frenzy, archers shoot flaming arrows into the Man and he explodes into flame, shooting trails of fiery sparks and screaming fireworks. An apocalyptic bacchanalia ensues, continuing long into the night. (ibid.)

In its appropriation, consciously or otherwise, of the notion of the scapegoat, where the nation's sins for the past year were offloaded to a goat which was then released into the wilderness (Leviticus 16:22), Burning Man – whose context is also that of the desert – has strong parallels with biblical ideas of ritual purity and cleanliness. Here, though, the scapegoat takes the form of the burning man himself, who makes good the perennial anxieties of the revellers through his own destruction. Further parallels may be discerned in the resemblance between the 'sheer hybrid strangeness and polyglot weirdness of the participants' (Wray) and the motley followers whom Jesus attracted as his disciples, themselves very much on the margins of society, and including tax-collectors, prostitutes and fishermen. The apotheosis of the festival, the destruction of the Man, has obvious connections with the ideas of atonement theology, where sin, misery and death are taken up and appropriated into God through the self-sacrifice of Christ on behalf of humanity. The Burning Man, hoisted aloft on a platform above the expectant crowd, even has his arms outstretched in emulation of crucifixion (some excellent full-colour photographs in the collection *Burning Man*, edited by Brad Wieners, strikingly illustrate the burning of the effigy, as well as other aspects of the whole event).

All of this suggests that there is in New Age phenomena much that deserves at the very least to be taken seriously by Christian theologians. Furthermore, it indicates that festivals, demonstrations and events at the outer edges of society, which are nominally just anti-capitalist or anti-corporate in their intentions, might have much more to offer, in the way of useful theological and spiritual resources, than may at first be apparent. Such events may be as genuinely liberating and theologically resonant as any church service, and possess considerably greater connectedness to cultural mores and responsible social aspirations as well. Here, in Burning Man, is a direct correlation between thinking, being and doing. When Matt Wray says that 'If there is a definitive meaning of the Man it is that there is no definitive meaning' ('Burning Man'), he is only articulating the paradox at the heart of the postmodern condition, which cannot deny the presence of meaning as such, located as this is in a complex heterogeneity of both dissonant and associative components. For Larry Harvey this gives rise to an extraordinary religious freedom:

> We do a lot of things priests do. Priests in any religion. Witness all the temples that have ever been built. Think of them as theme parks. These theme parks induce a certain kind of primal experience, a certain kind of excitement, a certain sort of passion. Except you have to pay to get into their theme parks. You have to pay an intellectual price. You have to accede to all kinds of doctrines whose essential purpose is to socially and economically control you. We just present the mystery. There stands the Man on his temple. Here it is folks. You don't have to believe in anything, by God. It's like pure faith, like revelation. It is entirely up to you to claim it for your own. (Wieners, p. 132)

Meaning comes through a glass darkly, and there is no reason to suppose that sacred truths should be any more subject to determination than the day-to-day complexities of secular life. Perhaps we should suppose that they might be less so. The idea that at the heart of religion and spirituality lies a mystery seems to me a promising one. It is an idea that many of the great religious thinkers have always taken very seriously. Simone Weil writes: 'There is a god. There is no God. Where is the problem? I am quite sure that there is a God in the sense that I am sure my love is no illusion. I am quite sure there is no God in the sense that I am sure there is nothing which resembles what I can conceive when I say that word' (*Waiting for God*, p. 32).

For many of us, weary of a culture of self-confident scientific rationalism, and made lonely through the absence of a God who cannot easily be relocated or identified, we are obliged to seek consolation elsewhere, in places where the divine appears to be mediated through unlikely avenues, or where our sense of it is that it both is and is not. Jenny Diski's book *Skating to Antarctica* intermingles, with great craft, inner and outer journeys into what becomes a single quest – the quest for meaning and truth in one of the author's central personal relationships. It is a work which implies that in the end transcendence is to be found in the ineffability and mystery of the Antarctic landscape, which points towards a world extending beyond itself, in all its ambiguous mingling of cloud, sky and sea:

> The scene from my cabin window was otherworldly . . . In the early hours of the morning, the light was pale silver, slightly misty. Half-close my eyes and there was nothing but a spectrum of grey, blue and off-white. It could have been bluey grey, greyish blue, hues of blue. There were huge bergs coming now. I suppose they were related. They came in waves. Three, four, but no, they were two big bergs. They must have broken off at the same time, or it could have been one big berg that split. On the horizon the cloud seemed to have settled down on to the sea and turned into another iceberg. It was impossible to tell what was cloud and what was berg in the distance. It looked fluffy, the same colour as the clouds higher up, only distinct, and squat, flat on the sea, but still cloudlike for all that. But it wasn't a cloud. Soon it turned into one . . . two separate bergs. It was all clouds and bergs, bergs and clouds. (p. 223)

The holistic movement always allows plenty of room for reflection of this nature which is deep, questioning and open-ended, and not only pointed towards the natural world, and in this respect it is to be applauded. Although alternative spirituality is sometimes shallow, it does not follow that this is always the case. There is frequently to be found there a serious search for God, however one defines that word, or for a religious and theological dimension to life, readily encouraged by holism, that is not confined to the remit of the established religions. A genuine and helpful search for the numinous goes beyond the vacuity of neatly constructed episodes of *The X-Files* into much looser, less easily packaged material, where the answers are not always to be found at the end of the story and where 'meaning' is multi-layered and open to several possible interpretations, or indeed to none at all. One recent treatment of ambivalent, mysterious spiritual forces is to be found in the novel *The Riders* by Tim Winton, which seems to me an excellent example of highly creative, 'alternative' spiritual writing. On one level this is a book about the increasingly desperate search by a deserted husband for the wife who has abandoned him and their daughter, her motives throughout the novel remaining unascertainable and implacable. At another level the work is a study of forces both human and inhuman, tangible and intangible, which cannot be understood, let alone controlled, by those who are brought into contact with them. Scully's search for answers is answered in the end only by the inexplicable – by confrontation with ghostly riders beside a ruined Irish castle who seem to encapsulate the futility of any quest for final definition:

> Scully smelled them, the riders and their horses. He recognised the blood and shit and sweat and fear of them, and he looked with them into the dead heart of the castle keep whose wings were bound east and west with snow-ghosted ash trees and ivy, whose rooks did not stir, whose light did not show and whose answer did not come. He knew them now and he saw that they would be here every night seen and unseen, patient, dogged, faithful in all weathers and all worlds, waiting for something promised, something that was plainly their due, but he knew that as surely as he felt Billie tugging on him, curling her fingers in his and pulling him easily away, that he would not be among them and must never be, in life or death. (Winton, p. 377)

Such writing properly acknowledges motivations that remain opaque to human beings, from phenomena which are both of, and set apart from, the world, while also allowing room for the fascinating mystery that is bound up with them. In that respect, and in his determination to avoid making facile connections or provide processed 'answers', in a context which – like all our contemporary contexts – is highly complex and thoroughly differentiated, Winton strikes a note that is clear and pure.

However, none of this open-mindedness and open-endedness takes away from the point made at the beginning of this chapter, that its commitment to inclusiveness makes New Age belief subject to critique on the grounds of a lack of discrimination in what it admits to its pantheon, and also that a historical or authoritative textual perspective is an important deficiency. Not just indiscriminate or irresponsible opinion, but the pathos of paranoia and obsessiveness, are apparent in the activities of several of those encountered by the journalist Jon Ronson. His book *Them: Adventures with Extremists* recounts the author's bizarre and frequently disturbing experiences of an assorted band of conspiracy theorists, pagans, self-appointed prophets and diverse ideological hardliners, who generally believe that the world is in thrall to an elite who run it from a mythic secret room. Ronson's stories lend plenty of anecdotal support to the claim made elsewhere by Žižek that 'the authentic Christian legacy is much too precious to be left to the fundamentalist freaks' (*The Fragile Absolute*, p. 2). The absence of textual veracity, meanwhile, may clearly be discerned in one of the most popular bibles of the holistic movement (surprisingly omitted by Bloom from his anthology), namely *The Celestine Prophecy* by James Redfield, which spent over 100 weeks on the *New York Times* bestseller list. This book, written in the form of a novel, is designed to impart nine insights about the nature of reality discovered by the anonymous hero in an archaic Mayan document. The author's message, in essence, is that the universe is composed of energy evolving into ever higher states of vibration: pure energy to hydrogen atoms, leading to molecules to organic matter to basic forms of life, and thence to humanity, finally culminating in a form of intelligent, non-corporeal being. The final stage allows people to direct their evolution consciously, a stage in which they acquire psychic energy through connecting with nature rather than through conflict with each other. As Redfield has it, the last fifty years have been the prelude to the beginning of the final countdown, as society at large reconnects with the mystical and the spiritual. This manifesto is reinforced in the mission statement to be found in the website established by Redfield and his followers at www.celestinevision.com:

> Our belief is that there is a growing worldwide interest in spirituality that is creating a new spiritual awareness and culture that will flourish in the new millennium . . . Ultimately we will realise that we are spiritual beings living in a spiritual world – a world that is precisely designed for the discovery and implementation of our most inspired dreams.

Further elaboration is offered in the April 2001 edition of the on-line *Celestine Journal*, accessed via the same website address:

> We are all now free to seriously pursue [*sic*] real spiritual experience and euphoria, the only real cure for the restlessness and feeling of incompleteness in one's life, and because of this a new, more advanced spiritual world view is forming. But while it forms, there will be a polarization between those who are pursuing and living this spiritual view, and those who are flailing around trying to hold on to the old purely materialistic life, taking this life in ever stranger directions. We have always to remember: even the most alienated person out there pursuing their directions with the tightest fury will eventually come round to what they are truly looking for. A new spiritual world will reorient human culture, if those of us who know hold the vision.

In its blandly optimistic and sweeping assumptions about the nature of human destiny and being, its egotism, its own coyly packaged materialism (the corporate website sits seriously at odds with the 'pure spirituality' it seeks to promote), its lack of any serious engagement with historical or cultural particularity, and its lack of engagement with textual tradition, of any major faith, the Celestine industry makes evident the fundamental weaknesses and ill-discipline of much of the New Age movement. It nevertheless articulates acutely felt needs on the part of people who are disoriented, fed up with materialism, and hungry for meaning and purpose in their lives. In order to reclaim resources for a new sort of theology, which has textual and historical integrity, but which responds adequately and sympathetically to people's real desires, we have to try to separate out the strengths and weaknesses of this diverse and fascinating collection of spiritualities.

I would suggest that in order to qualify as authentically meaningful, holistic belief and practice should incarnate the following characteristics. It should be collective, democratic and participative, and look towards the needs of whole communities, rather than exclusively individualistic, preferably with a marked sense of social, political and ecological responsibility. It should be tradition-based, with a strong sense of its own historical development, with all the compromises and lessons this has involved (whether we are talking about ancient Druidic belief or witchcraft) in the process. And it should remain generously broad-minded while still discriminating in the choices it makes, and be subject too to firm policing, so that evidently harmful or dangerous doctrines are excluded from its forum. This may not be easy; one of the major deficiencies of a decentralised network of beliefs is that, unlike the churches, there are no obvious officers to administer rules or pluck out dissenters. In jettisoning federalism and a centralised authority, for the sake of freedom of self-expression, one may also have to be prepared to relinquish clear and observable guidelines for regulation. In this respect, the strong traditions and canons of the Church, forged in the white heat of long theological controversy, begin to seem altogether less about authoritarianism and more about administrative common sense. There are, it seems, two sides to every story.

It may be that there are other criteria, overlooked here, that will help to identify the holistic resources we are looking for. Nevertheless, those that I identify might I think – in the right circumstances: that is, properly policed and mediated – result in valuable spiritualities that have something positive and beneficial to say to Christian theology.

Of course we need to guard against that in the New Age movement which is ephemeral, naïve, hypocritically materialist or selfishly individualistic, and there is much to be found here that is all those things and more. However, there is in addition so much diversity, originality and energy in the movement, that one cannot help but acknowledge the value of its critique of secular postmodernity, even while recognising its own origins in that same postmodern culture whose defining characteristics it largely shares. We must now hope for a rehabilitation of the traditional theological enterprise, whose greatest insights remain unheard but are still to be profoundly cherished. In the next chapter I want to propose that theology at its most potent offers what perhaps nothing in the holistic movement can duplicate to the same degree: a concern with individual and communal salvation alike which encompasses the whole world; and a commitment to economic, social and political critique on a scale which is utopian in the best sense of the word. A truly cosmological, as opposed to an ethical or individualistic metaphysics, tends to be lacking in much holistic literature. Accordingly, we shall look at some representative theologies that seem to offer ways of conceptualising life in its totality which are still promising, still valuable, and which – precisely because they are so deeply engaged with secular thought – have something more than superficial to offer the secular world.

## CHAPTER 4

# Towards a Secular Theology

In 1998 I attended a conference in Cambridge whose aim was to envisage new ways of conceptualising Christian worship and liturgy. One of the main speakers and participants at that event was the writer P. D. James, who was at the time a prominent member of the Church of England's Liturgical Commission. In her recent autobiography, Baroness James has referred to her experience of encountering theological literature at that conference, and to her disappointment at finding anything on the publishers' displays that was intelligible or – by inference – credible:

> Between lectures I looked at some of the theological books on sale in the hall. Most seemed to me totally incomprehensible. Obviously doctrinally and philosophically they would be well above my understanding, but it seemed that the sentences themselves were incomprehensible, a string of polysyllabic words strung together from which I could get no meaning. Theology, like other professions, has its own obscurantism. The problem is surely that theology should impinge on the lives of ordinary non-theologians if it is to have influence. Surely it can sometimes be written in language the intelligent lay man or woman can understand. (*Time to Be in Earnest*, p. 173)

At this point, and not without shame, I must come clean: as one of the publishers responsible, I acknowledge my own blame for the impenetrability of a number of the books she describes. It is comforting for theological publishers (and this is as much about self-preservation as anything else) to assume that people at large still have an appetite for poring over highly complex deconstructions of traditional Christian faith, when in fact the demography and the sales figures – at least, outside seminaries, universities and college courses – might suggest otherwise. For years several well-established religious publishing houses have considered themselves to be the barometer of people's innermost spiritual needs, being deeply preoccupied in their output with the kinds of Christianity that they assume their readers most practise and discuss. This assumption bypasses the fact that society has changed unrecognisably since the *Honest to God* debates of the early sixties. It overlooks the total secularisation of culture, and fails to get to grips with the fact that for most people the critical question is no longer what kinds of Christianity they need, but whether in fact they need *any kind of Christianity at all.* Long gone are the days when non-believers read Tillich or Niebuhr because the Christian thinking of those writers was perceived to have wider relevance and application. Yet several publishers, as providers of food for the soul, are still fixated on ecclesiological fish and chips, when everyone round about is voraciously consuming chicken tikka masala, now served up with an increasingly desacralised degree of culinary sophistication.

The decline of traditional religious publishing is a microcosm of the decline of theology – in terms of its actual felt connection to people's lives – more generally. On the one hand society has broken free of any real theological connection (with the consequences we have seen in the last two chapters), and on the other hand theology has, as a result, retreated into a tranche of defensive positions where it feels more secure. This means into rejection of an objective divinity, or a self-absorbed detachment from the 'real world', or even into a kind of triumphal self-assertion where, against all the odds, it proclaims itself to be the guardian of the anticipated Holy City, the new Jerusalem, of which secular communities are manifestly flawed approximations. ('What emerges is a contemporary theological project made possible by the self-conscious superficiality of today's secularism', *Radical Orthodoxy*, p. 1.) In most cases there is a singular lack of *positive* engagement with the culture of postmodernity, and a singular lack of desire to acknowledge that the secular world is where all of us live out our hopes, disappointments and dreams, and that this is the context where the particularity of life, for all its misanthropy and misadventure, is envisioned. P. D. James laments the inaccessibility of much theological literature; but this is not just a superficial problem about language (which, in its complexity and over-reliance on jargon, *is* sometimes thrown up as a smokescreen to guard against loss of influence) but also of a fundamental shift of conceptuality. When theologians talk about such concepts as 'sin', 'grace', 'atonement' and 'redemption', such traditionalist notions sound risible, anachronistic and ridiculously absolutist to the ears of the pick-and-mix generation of young postmoderns. Why on earth get fixated on only one solution? As Nik Cohn reminds us, 'One God leads to another. Some days, travelling the city, it seems there's a different version of the Almighty on every street corner. Familiar favourites like the Jehovah's Witnesses and the Plymouth Brethren compete for space with Rastafarians, Odinists, Wiccans, Zoroastrians . . . The republic is a babel. It speaks in tongues' (*Yes We Have No*, p. 327).

Alistair McFadyen attempts in an interesting recent book to reclaim some lost ground for traditional theological conceptuality, and concentrates on the notion of sin as offering a promising test case for the rejuvenation of constructive God-talk in society. He first responsibly acknowledges that we live in a culture which is fundamentally secular, 'which affirms the world's integrity and independence from any external, non-worldly reality so that it may be understood in its own terms, without immediate or explicit reference to God' (*Bound to Sin*, p. 6). This is a situation that he describes as one of 'pragmatic atheism', where God is allowed only into the gaps where the educative power of secular discourse and secular rationality is less potent than in the mainstream:

> Hence, for example, the doctrine of creation ceases to function as a means for affirming the presence and activity of God in and through the very integrity of the world's natural order and processes as these may be described through the natural sciences. Instead, creation is evaporated to the point of God's initial responsibility for the natural world. After which, ceasing to have any 'natural' function, God is irrelevant to the task of understanding the natural order and processes of the world. (p. 7)

In a world in which God is effectively missing from 'every discipline of interpretation, analysis, explanation and action' (p. 8), and where secular discourse operates on its own terms in these areas, atheism is the prevalent attitude which to all practical intents and purposes we live out in our culture. No matter what personal beliefs and religious disposition we may profess, *de facto* we live as if there were no God. This is as true of the other major faith traditions as it is of Christianity, however they may organise themselves internally in relation to culture. The overarching context is one where in the public domain faith in God makes no practical difference to how the world is lived and understood. McFadyen is absolutely certain about the weight of the challenge that this poses: theology needs to show that reference to God still has explanatory and descriptive power, and that it provides a means of more truthfully configuring reality than the psychologising explanations of contemporary Western culture. For McFadyen the all-pervasiveness of sin (a 'universally extensive reality', p. 49), which he explores through the concrete pathologies of the Nazi Holocaust and child abuse, offers a way into affirming the beneficent action of the trinitarian God in the world. Secularity is thus at once affirmed and profoundly complemented by the Christian hope – and in an important sense transcended by it (p. 53). Adhering to basically traditional Christian notions of existential redemption and liberation, McFadyen sees in the cross and resurrection of Jesus the answer to pathologies of sin. Despite the damage and brokenness the latter cause, they are countered by a dynamic, salvific action in which God moves towards us in Christ (p. 211). For McFadyen sin is a turning away from God, an idolatrous counter-dynamic that gives primacy to other forces in the world (p. 224); conversely, he finds in Christian worship a way to orient the self towards a source of divine energy which properly becomes normative for goodness and value and which results in transfiguration through joy (p. 238).

McFadyen's emphasis on bringing Christian theology into direct engagement with secular thought is welcome, and his attempts to wrestle with the extremely complex and controversial problematic of abuse and of genocide are admirable. Despite this, there will be those who remain unconvinced by his prioritisation of Christian hope, over secular alternatives, apparently by means of worshipping communities within which sin is countermanded by joy. How does this *really* get to grips, they may ask, with the concrete nature of evil as it is manifested in the world, and how does exposure to what he calls the dynamic energy of God really help anybody at all in real terms? Furthermore, at a time when organised Christian worship is diminishing, how realistic is his emphasis on joyful worship as the viable way forward? In fact, where *are* these joyous communities? McFadyen is a sensitive and sympathetic writer, but there is a suspicion that his abstract theological conceptuality will leave some people feeling frustrated and lacking concrete answers. Furthermore, I am not at all sure how helpful the traditional language of sin remains in a context where such conceptuality has very little continuing resonance. Might we not be better off talking perhaps about 'ignorance', and the necessity of addressing its damaging consequences in ways that educate people into an appropriate and sensitive condition of self-knowledge, generosity and hope?

Pragmatic atheism is all very well, but if rationalist solutions to particular problems function with practical coherence (so that evil and ignorance – or 'sin' – are understood psychologically, and are addressed correspondingly, either by way of rehabilitation or punishment, and the social order is maintained thereby), then why do we need to keep God or theology in the picture *at all*? Why do we need to keep hold of God, if for all practical purposes God has gone AWOL? Can't we be brave enough to come up with our own answers to the problems we encounter in life? Isn't it sheer insecurity or immaturity that causes us to cling on to the idea that we have qualitative preference over the birds of the air and the lilies of the field (Matthew 6:26–30) in the hierarchy of the created order?

Bertrand Russell considered belief in God to be craven and contemptible, and this is often the form in which so-called protest atheism mounts its bitterest attack on religious or theological conceptuality. For Russell, religion evinced a deeply unattractive kind of special pleading: 'When you hear people in church debasing themselves and saying that they are miserable sinners, and all the rest of it, it seems . . . not worthy of self-respecting human beings. We ought to stand up and look the world frankly in the face' (*Why I Am Not A Christian*, p. 26).

A more considered, but no less absolutist, view of human autonomy is aired at one point in John Fowles' novel *The Magus*, where the narrator, Maurice Conchis, describes to a young English schoolmaster, who is the book's main protagonist, the highly rationalistic approach to life that he adopted when he was himself a young man: 'My whole approach was scientific, medical, classifying. I was conditioned by a kind of ornithological approach to man. I thought in terms of species, behaviours, observations' (p. 269). However, in a development that thoroughly endorses the propensity of the human spirit to direct itself (or be directed) towards the ineffable and the mysterious, Conchis eventually is confronted by something that shatters his complacent rationalism and faith in scientific endeavour (the characteristic optimism of post-Enlightenment modernism). He recounts his travelling into the heart of the Scandinavian fir-forests of north Norway in order to conduct an ornithological field-trip, where he stays with an educated farmer, Gustav, who shares his passion for birds. It soon becomes clear that not everything at Seidevarre is as it first seems. It emerges that living in secret on an isolated spit of land which runs down to the river, a little south of the farm, is Gustav's brother Henrik, who has gone insane. Gustav has taken over responsibility for his brother's family, while Henrik, who lives in ascetic isolation, and is now almost completely blind, is totally dependent on his relatives for survival. The kind of insanity with which Henrik is afflicted soon becomes apparent: he has retreated into (as Conchis first sees it) religious mania.

Conchis, who in Paris has founded a 'Society of Reason', and is a doctor, determines to save Henrik by examining his eyes and psychoanalysing him. Approaching Henrik one day on the spit, Conchis is forcefully rejected, and almost killed, as his intended interlocutor pursues him with an axe. Initially it seems incredible to Conchis, who has made his getaway after a narrow escape, that 'a man should reject medicine, reason, science so violently' (p. 267). But a later, startling development utterly shakes his self-confidence that these disciplines are necessarily able to order and encompass reality by themselves. Looking out for Henrik from a distance, Conchis and Gustav hear a cry:

> For a moment I thought it must be some bird, but then I knew it could only be Henrik. I looked towards the farmstead. I could see Gustav had stopped, was standing outside, listening. Another cry came. It was dragged out, the cry of someone who is calling a great distance. I walked across the grass to Gustav. 'Is he in trouble?' I asked. He shook his head, and remained staring out at the dark shadow of Seidevarre across the moon-grey water. What was he calling? Gustav said, 'Do you hear me? I am here.' And then the two cries, with an interval between, came again and I could make out the Norwegian words. *'Hører du mig? Jeg er her.'* Henrik was calling to God. (p. 268)

Eventually the two men come in sight of Henrik, who is standing out in the river, at the very tip of the shingle spit. What follows is an epiphany which destroys all of Conchis' previous certainties about the nature of reality and of the human capacity to describe it:

> Out in midstream there were long low banks of mist. As we watched, he called. *'Hører du mig?'* With great force. As if to someone several miles away, on the invisible far bank. A long pause. Then, *'Jeg er her.'* I trained my glasses on him. He was

> standing, legs astride, his staff in his hand, biblically. There was silence. A black silhouette in the glittering current. Then we heard Henrik say one word. Much more quietly. It was '*Takk*.' The Norwegian for 'thanks.' I watched him. He stepped back a pace or two out of the water, and knelt on the shingle. We heard the sounds of the stones as he moved. He still faced the same way. His hands by his side. It was not an attitude of prayer, but a watching on his knees. Something was very close to him, as visible to him as Gustav's dark head, the trees, the moonlight on the leaves around us, was to me. I would have given ten years of my life to have been able to look out there from the north, from inside his mind. I did not know what he was seeing, but I knew it was something of such power, such mystery, that it explained all. And of course Henrik's secret flashed in on me, almost like some reflection of the illumination that was flashing in on him. He was not waiting to meet God. He was meeting God; and had been meeting him probably for many years. He was not waiting for some certainty. He lived in it. (p. 269)

This extraordinary and revelatory mystery bursts upon the narrator with cathartic force:

> In a flash of terrible light all our explanations, all our classifications and derivations, our aetiologies, suddenly appeared to me like a thin net. That great passive monster, reality, was no longer dead, easy to handle. It was full of a mysterious vigour, new forms, new possibilities. The net was nothing, reality burst through it. (p. 270)

What Conchis comes to see is that his 'explanations' are nothing so much as a construction erected for his own convenience and self-protection, and that something far more elusive, yet far more profound and far more extensive, lies beyond it. Not all of us are able to experience God in the form of direct encounter, as Henrik did in Fowles' novel, but many of us nevertheless have some sense of the numinous, the mysterious, and the other, which stretches beyond our own immediate vistas. This notion of the importance of mystery, to which I have already drawn attention, is one to which atheists are rarely prepared to give due weight, and it offers as I see it a far richer way of configuring ourselves – our natures and our destinies – than many rationalist, Enlightenment categories are generally prepared to allow. There is often to be detected in these accounts (and Russell is no exception here: indeed, he is more singularly paradigmatic than most, given his own personal failings – see Ray Monk's illuminating biography, *Bertrand Russell: The Spirit of Solitude*) a cynicism in the rejection of God and the transcendent which says rather more about their progenitors and their circumstantial prejudices than they do about the inadequacy of a religious sensibility to propose credible solutions to complex problems. While there is plenty to be gained from a questioning and intelligent agnosticism, it seems to me regrettable that those who absolutely reject the Other can sometimes be so coruscating, when reality is a good deal more complex than any single philosophical or metaphysical position could be likely to encompass. After all, why should human modes of analysis show us all that there is? The nature of reality depends on where and how you look at it. For example, birds are able to determine colours that are invisible to human beings. The perspective of the world depends on whether you look at it from above, from below, or sideways, from the air or on the ground. In these conditions, can it make any sense to say that only one perspective is 'true', and that there is no room for different layers of ambiguity?

Of course, it might be countered that all the evil in the world, and God's apparent absence from it, leave little choice but to reject any notion of a beneficent creator, whose existence in these sordid circumstances becomes nonsensical. Yet Christian theology claims precisely that God is *not* absent from the world, whatever the world thinks, and that God cared so much about creation that he entered it in human form and died within it, in order to identify completely with suffering, death, and the general malignancy of the created order. There is little that is overt in secular thought, or for that matter in New Age thinking, which offers a systematic remedy to the world's ills that is configured in terms of this kind of universal salvation. The trouble is that theologians are sometimes reluctant to admit that all the cynicism and nastiness apparent in the world are still, because it is God's world, worthy of serious engagement and conversation on terms other than Christian ones, even though secular terms of reference might seem strange, superficial or off-putting. Ambiguity, attentiveness and mystery – these are some of the conceptualities which I think would help to bring Christian theology back into contact with the secular provisionalities and inadequacies that so characterise postmodernity.

Theologians often see the eucharist as the mode, *par excellence*, whereby the mystery of God is mediated to human beings. The breaking of the bread and the sharing of the wine are regarded as the greatest symbols that there are of Christ's continuing presence in the world through the workings of Holy Spirit among the community of believers. The eucharist epitomises relationship: and for the theologian T. J. Gorringe, in the celebration of the eucharist 'we rehearse the question of what it means to become human' (*The Sign of Love*, p. 87). Gorringe, in one of the most attractive liturgical theologies around, further understands the eucharist as a fundamentally *political* sacrament, in that it represents not so much a re-enactment of the Last Supper as the articulation of Jesus' radical outlook during the entire course of his ministry. According to this picture the Feeding of the Five Thousand is interpreted as miraculous because, through Jesus' generous example, people were shamed into sharing with one another, resulting in plenty of sustenance for all. The eucharist which 'comes out of the great feedings' is thus 'a sign act of the need to share what we have' (*The Education of Desire*, p. 110). Liturgical practice, for Gorringe, therefore becomes a symbol of identification with resistance to economic oppression – through the elimination of poverty – and to unbridled global consumption. 'To become a burning sign', he writes, 'it needs to be related to action' (ibid.). Such heartfelt identification with the concrete problems of the world is admirable, and Gorringe is one British theologian who has been prepared to wrestle consistently with its travails in all of his writings. The trouble is that celebration of the eucharist is such an intrinsically *churchly* action. Located specifically within church buildings, it is furthermore so closely associated with the fabric of the Church as an institution (a largely irrelevant and often discredited institution, as we have seen), that many find it alienating, boring or simply incomprehensible. Sadly it represents not so much a sign of radical action as of nonsensical or intimidating ritualism. In an era when many people – harassed for time, or just plain harassed – would rather spend their Sunday mornings queuing at the food counters of Tesco or Sainsbury's than singing hymns or partaking of Holy Communion, the eucharist is unlikely to make a significant comeback as the chief instrument of Christian revival, or of a rejuvenated Christian conceptuality of how to combat world hunger.

Ours is the age of what has been called 'time squeeze' or even 'time famine'. We are all more conscious of time than ever before, to the degree that it has become a second consumer currency: we invest it, save it and spend it in the same way as we do money. British men work the longest hours in Western Europe, their professional women counterparts are rapidly catching up, and – according to the *Observer* (27 May 2001) – lift manufacturers complain that they are having to replace 'close door' buttons more regularly, worn out through impatient stabbing. But work cannot take all the blame for the time famine. People are generally much more demanding of themselves. Active parenting, exercise, demanding and fast-paced relationships, learning new technology, making space for proper holidays, doing creative cooking, taking care of their elders, and sleeping, all result in a time squeeze.

This isolates a central problem for the emergence of a credible postmodern theology. Since people no longer have the time or the inclination to explore the sense of mystery in church, and are doing so as we have seen in startlingly decreasing numbers, how is it possible to take theology out into the world, on to the streets, into the football terraces, the supermarkets and the garage forecourts? How do we talk theologically, in these contexts, in a way that *genuinely makes sense*, and which has resonance with what people really think and feel? In the first place, as I have suggested, theology needs to engage respectfully with the realities with which it is confronted. It needs to look, listen, and learn from others, rather than perpetually tell them what to think, how to worship, how to come back to Church, where all the answers miraculously will be revealed. It needs to stop treating people like wayward children and arrogantly appropriating to itself all the solutions. If religious sensibility is by no means absent from the shopping arcades, the town centres, the airports and the motorways, then why should God be any less accessible there than in the abandoned churches or among depleted congregations? I contend in this book that God is to be found precisely in those places where churchpeople might often prefer that God is not. That is, in the places where people dream of liberation and release (whether through Lottery winnings, or promotion at work, or sex, or engagement with characters in a TV soap): in the neglected questing sensibilities and transcendent aspirations, in fact, of the generations of the lost. Worship needs to be deregulated, and relocated outside as much as inside the confines of church buildings. The sacred might then be discerned and disseminated in many different forms – in stories in movies, books and television; in face-to-face encounter and discussion; in a re-evaluation and appreciation of the natural world; in direct political action and the activities of Christian NGOs; in aesthetics and the arts. If the essential tenets of Christianity are true, that God so identified with and loved the world that he came to redeem it, then the death of formalised Christian worship in this land takes nothing away from the integrity of the fundamentals; neither does it subtract from the power, veracity and compassion of God's will to furnish us with other possibilities. Do we need to partake of the bread and the wine to be Christians if we have genuine Christian sensibility? If we live generous and ethically determined lives, and respond to our fellow citizens and our world in the self-giving spirit of the gospels, do we need to be in church to prove ourselves Christian? Is regimented worship necessary to understand the nature of forgiveness, charity or compassion? Traditionalists may say that to move in this direction is a denial of everything that makes Christianity distinctive; that it points towards a vague, desacralised and decentralised Gnosticism, where 'anything goes'. But I am not saying that anything goes – simply that what we now have is not enough to bring people to a true appreciation of that sacred and mysterious presence which is greater than ourselves. That essentialism is what we urgently need to rediscover if we are not finally to be consumed by the very processes of consumption towards which we now rush so dangerously.

My contention is thus that *within secular culture* are to be found those resources for a reciprocal exchange, so that theology can see how much there is there that is to be profoundly cherished and valued; while the secular sphere may see in turn how a concertedly articulated reverence for the mysterious and the transcendent can greatly nourish and lend meaning to human life. In some ways we are close here to the thinking of the Catholic theologian Karl Rahner, for whom all the time, and in everyday ways, human beings reach out beyond themselves and their finite existence, towards that which offers the prospect that the world might actually make sense. The horizon of possibility which opens out to us as goodness, truth and being is identified by Rahner as the Christian God. But since Christian faith may not necessarily be acknowledged by people, even though the capacity to awake to goodness is present, through grace, in every human nature, Rahner felt able to refer to this capacity as 'anonymous Christianity'. For Rahner, human transcendental experience is perhaps more than anything else about the capacity to hope, often (and this idea, as we will see later, is also explored by Andrei Tarkovsky) where hope seems groundless:

> There is a man who is absolutely lonely, who finds all the right elements of life pale shadows; for whom all trustworthy handholds take him into the infinite distance, and who does not run away from this loneliness but treats it with ultimate hope . . . There is one who suddenly notices how the tiny trickle of his life wanders through the wilderness of the banality of existence, apparently without aim and with the heartfelt fear of complete exhaustion. And yet he hopes, he knows not how, that this trickle will find the infinite expanse of the ocean, even though it may still be covered by the grey sands which seem to extend for ever before him. (*The Spirit*

> *in the Church*, pp. 18–22, quoted in Karl-Heinz Weger, *Karl Rahner: An Introduction to his Theology*, pp. 92–3)

Thus transcendence lies not just – or perhaps primarily – in finding God in happiness or joy or gratitude, or in contexts formally ratified as 'Christian', but also in loneliness, depression, loss and grief. More will be said about this – and about a responsible acknowledgement of negativity and of the apparent absence of 'answers' – in Chapters 5 and 6.

As I have noted in Chapter 1, Daniel Hardy speaks of divine wisdom coming to us through the rainbow disciplines, from outside as well as inside the Church, and looks towards a kind of 'wisdom theology' which is mediated towards us through the several manifestations of economic, social-political, technological and cultural life, in a great variety of different forms. For Hardy, faith is and can never be concentrated in just one place:

> The Bible is a vast history of God engaging with the people in special ways; the Church is a complex of people faithful in very different situations through history; beliefs testify to God's purposes for all people throughout history; and even certainty is a life-process, not 'sudden' and 'complete'. These things give a hint of the breadth, spread-out-ness and time-involving character of God's work and the Christian faith that responds to it. (*Finding the Church*, p. 110)

Hardy's view is that the wisdom of God – the 'movement of God's truth and holiness' (p. 109) – comes to human beings over the extended course of time. But as he sees it there is another kind of 'extensity' at work here, namely 'the situations in which they live'. This suggests that God is to be found in the curry house as much as the chapel, and that secular life is a rich and abundant location for aspects of divinity. Fergus Kerr recognises as much in his excellent book *Immortal Longings*, where his analysis of the works of six recent secular philosophers reveals 'how important theological motifs and considerations are in the development and articulation of their projects' (p. 164). Hardy's and Kerr's writings imply also that it is through direct engagement with secular life and thought that increased understanding, on both sides, is going to come. Alistair McFadyen is one theologian who speaks directly to the condition of postmodernity in connection with the specific pathologies of abuse and genocide. But if his notion of joyful worship – like Gorringe's related emphasis on eucharistic efficacy – seems somewhat intangible in relation to these stark realities, there are other writers who address perhaps even more directly the issues that are of universal concern in human life. I do detect in some recent theology a tendency to retreat too easily into liturgy and the complexities of formalised ritual and worship, when faced by people's incomprehension, inattentiveness and derision – or into claims like that made by William Cavanaugh, that 'the body of the state is a simulacrum, a false copy, of the Body of Christ' (*Radical Orthodoxy*, p. 182). My feeling is that this is unfortunate, exclusive, and is moving in the wrong direction. I would suggest that theology needs to be more sinewy and fluid, less rigid and liturgically deterministic, in its appeal to those – the 'godfearers' and religious sympathisers – who cry for recognition in the wilderness, and should properly start with the world as it is before telling us how it should be. In this connection, the warning of Rowan Williams (echoing the famous dictum of Wittgenstein's *Tractatus* – 'Whereof one cannot speak thereof one must be silent') seems especially apt:

> Talking theologically, talking of how religion avoids becoming the most dramatically empty and power-obsessed discourse imaginable, is necessary and very difficult. It is out to make the discourse of faith and worship both harder and more authoritative (more transparent to its origin). And to do this it needs to know when it has said what it can say and when it is time to shut up. (*On Christian Theology*, p. 15)

One important group of theologians who are passionately and comprehensibly concerned about the specific circumstances of the world as we live in it are those influenced by insights from liberation theology and from contemporary political discourse. In their respective books *Grace and Mortgage* and *On Human*

*Worth* Peter Selby and Duncan B. Forrester directly address the questions of debt and inequality, and both are thoroughly engaged with what they see as crucial issues of social and economic policy. Forrester speaks for both when he writes that theology 'needs to address the policymakers, and the citizenry, and the church with a message that is often disturbing and challenging . . . This kind of theology is rooted in the real world and its issues and its suffering. It is intended to arouse conviction and lead to action. It cares for people more than for intellectual coherence, or literary elegance, or academic respectability' (p. 72). This determination to take a 'preferential option for the poor' – the famous mantra of liberation theology – is mirrored in the work of many of the Christian aid agencies, like Oxfam, CAFOD and Christian Aid, who are thoroughly committed to improving the living conditions of the economically, politically, or socially oppressed, keeping firmly in mind gospel notions of justice, equality and liberation. Such theology in action is admirably engaged and committed, and strongly informed by ideas of communitarianism, praxis and collective responsibility. It also calls for *personal* responsibility. For Selby, human beings, and especially Christians, are required to make a direct personal decision as to whether or not 'they will continue to collude with structures that so manifestly destroy life and elevate money from being an instrument to being a divinity' (p. 162).

A similar sense of communitarian conviction informing personal life is evident in the work of David Matzko McCarthy, who in his recent book *Sex and Love in the Home* relates questions of sex and relationships between individuals to wider relationships within whole communities and households. Relocating sexuality in the social space of everyday lives, McCarthy manages convincingly to show that the meaning of intimacy and relationships lies not in some magnificent grand narrative but precisely in their ordinariness: 'sexual practices cultivate a deep sense of belonging and identity because they are part of the day-to-day connections that carry our lives' (p. 208). This is a more radical message than it might seem, because, as McCarthy indicates, challenging the notion that domestic life is a purely personal commodity, and situating the home in the wider operations of a whole neighbourhood, involves a sustained critique of market capitalism. While the market 'requires that our desires be nomadic, that our longings never find a resting place', sustaining a rationality which 'offers few interesting places to settle down', the open household, by contrast, 'is open to unmanageable and interminable forms of gift-exchange and reciprocity' (p. 213). Contrasting the notions of a socially engaged and neighbourly household (which is open to wider networks of friendship and mutuality of support), with a private family (which is not, and which wrongly supposes that human life is 'completed' through a single, central relationship), McCarthy conceives of domestic life as a socially and economically productive place, where the simple matters of the everyday are 'key forms of resistance to the dominating market' (p. 214). By developing thoroughly theological ideas of mutuality, reciprocity and communion, while at the same time working within recognisable parameters of secular social theory, McCarthy is able to point towards a notion of human community which is altruistic, self-giving and reflective of divine love.

Theology such as this, which is concerned with the preoccupations of whole communities rather than with individuals, often has an authority and a radicalism behind it which other, exclusively personalist, accounts are lacking. As we have seen, a notable failing of some New Age literature and thought is its thoroughgoing emphasis on the individual and on personal growth and development, with the result that collective action scarcely gets a look in at all. When theologians challenge injustice, when they call for committed engagement with poverty, when they articulate a creative response to the demands of community living, they are reflecting in their own words some of the central principles of the gospel texts. They are writing, speaking and teaching in a manner that has integrity. Yet churchpeople who are more interested in the order for Evensong, or the form of worship, or their place on church committees, or their advancement within the church hierarchy, are oriented less towards what they are supposed to be there for – us, the people of God – than towards their own priorities. As Daniel Hardy reminds us, there are forms of learning appropriate to Christians which are not specific only to faith and theology (*Finding the Church*, p. 108). Theologians need to engage with the world if the world is to engage with them, and that means doing so in a way which people can hear and with which they can empathise. In this connection, a capacity responsibly to conceptualise communal life is extremely important, especially when impending ecological calamity makes it incumbent on all of us to take collective, as well as individual, responsibility for our continuing tendency to view creation simply as 'raw material for technological exploitation' (Kerr, p. 163).

If an assumption of collective responsibility is a central component of what I believe good theology to be, does this leave a gap for theologies that speak with power and conviction to wholly individual concerns? After all, part of the success of holistic thought – even though it may be weak on cosmology – is its capacity precisely to address people's particular desires, fears and aspirations. It would be regrettable if the individual were altogether subsumed into a theological conceptuality located predominantly only at the wider social and political level of human life and activity. One might reasonably ask where theology can be found when a youngster dehydrates and collapses on a club dancefloor; or when an aeroplane crashes, and media pundits agonise over the meaninglessness and waste of it all; or when earthquakes erase whole villages. Less dramatically, but no less significantly to those concerned, we might ask what theology has to say to all those who are angry, alienated, depressed, or who for one reason or another feel victimised or hopeless. Theology has always focused above all on hope, exactly as Rahner does. It offers a highly developed metaphysic which proposes that God so completely identified with the created world that he entered it in human form, suffered and died, and was resurrected in order to demonstrate conclusively that despair and death were not the end. Furthermore, Jesus always had time for those on the periphery, for the prostitutes, the tax collectors, the reviled, the poor, and the manifestly working class – indeed he made a point of prioritising such people, and was impatient with all kinds of hypocrisy and social snobbery. Death, indubitably, and often hardship, are part of the human condition, as we all know, but as John Bowker observes in his discussion of entropy, there is more to it than that. Death is actually a fundamental prerequisite for life itself:

> It is not possible to arrive at life except via the route of death. That means, in turn, that the price which has to be paid for any organisation of energy in a universe of this kind is very high indeed. It is not possible to acquire new energy out of nowhere from nothing . . . What is happening is that available energy is constantly being used and reorganised to build whatever there is – planets or plants, suns or sons. But as energy is used, so it is increasingly unavailable to do further work. (*The Meanings of Death*, p. 216)

This opens up the possibility of a theology of creative sacrifice (to which I've already alluded in connection with the Strugatskys' *Roadside Picnic*), since it is only through life making way, through death, for other life to begin, that human beings are enabled to continue as we do:

> 'For greater love hath no one than this, that he lay down his life for his friends' . . . That, consummately, is what Jesus did on the cross. But it is what countless others have also done through the long centuries of human history. (p. 227)

Bowker knows all too well that 'death kills. And grief knows it', and that any ontology of death needs to be extremely careful to guard against offensive complacency, false optimism, or superficial piety. But he is sensitive and imaginative enough to state that, while the crucifixion might represent the deep truth that you cannot have life in our universe without death, the idea of the resurrection might at the same time indicate that there is not death without the consequence of there also being life:

> All the evidence of the universe points in that direction: you cannot have life without death; but where you do have death, there you can have life. In the context of a universe of this kind, the resurrection is not particularly surprising . . . And

> this life, this risen life, has clearly led the way to a new limit of possibility. (p. 229)

Theology is about, or ought to be about, exactly this, whether it is orientated towards people individually or collectively – new horizons of hope and possibility and transformation. Cynicism, alienation, consumerism, despair and rejection – even death – are perhaps not all that there is. Theology posits that there is room for an alternative view, and good theology takes that view out into the world in a way that is accessible and genuinely liberative. At the same time, good and responsible theology takes on board the fact that despair, alienation and rampant individualism are real and pressing and have their own sorts of dynamic. The best kind of theology listens and learns from what it hears and sees on the course of its travels. It makes use, with critical self-awareness and some sense of its own acute limitations – since it is very far from being an exact science – of certain valuable resources which it encounters along the way. It acknowledges the transcendent in the cinema, at the food counter and in shopping malls. It knows that God is a mystery, and cannot be circumscribed, prescribed, controlled, or limited to one location as distinct from another. It knows that God is also a story, communicated within our own separate life stories and histories. Above all it knows that since it is *of* the world, it must be *in* the world to articulate any genuinely engaged and credible message of metaphysical involvement in human affairs. That is why I am calling it 'secular theology'. And it is to some of the places where those resources might most interestingly be located that I want to turn in the next two chapters.

# CHAPTER 5

# Resources for a Secular Theology (1): Fiction

I have already alluded to a number of secular novels which communicate ideas of transcendence in a powerful and energising way. It is time to examine the practice of storytelling in more detail, since in the process of telling stories I believe we have one of the most valuable tools at our disposal for the reinvigoration of theological language and conceptuality. In one of the best studies – in my view – yet published on the subject of theology and story, *Speaking in Parables*, Sallie McFague recognises the potential and integrity of what she calls intermediary or parabolic theology:

> A theology that is informed by parables is necessarily a risky and open-ended kind of reflection. It recognizes not only the inconclusiveness of all conceptualization when dealing with matters between God and human beings . . . but also the pain and scepticism – the dis-ease – of such reflection. Theology of this sort is not neat and comfortable; but neither is the life with and under God of which it attempts to speak. The parables accept the complexity and ambiguity of life as lived in the world and insist that it is in this world that God makes his gracious presence known. A theology informed by the parables can do no less – and no more. (p. 7)

McFague offers an important counterbalance here to much

contemporary systematic theology (what she calls 'second-order' theology), which tends to begin with creeds and doctrines and then only later move on to the lives of those who are supposed to be their recipients. Too much of this kind of theology talks about joy, or rapture, or gets lost in liturgical obscurity, and it therefore relinquishes its authenticity in a forbidding set of conceptual abstractions which have little or no connectedness to life as it is lived. McFague is right to insist on the primacy of experience, out of which the integrity of belief becomes felt and known:

> We all love a good story because of the basic narrative quality of human experience; in a sense, any story is about ourselves, and a good story is good precisely because somehow it rings true to human life. Human life is not marked by instantaneous rapture and easy solutions. Life is tough . . . We love stories, then, because our lives are stories and we recognize in the attempts of others to move, temporally and painfully, our own story. (pp. 138–9)

McFague insists that in the parables of Jesus, which embrace the power of the secular and the everyday, we see things as they are meant to be seen. Through the stories of Jesus, and Jesus himself as *the* Story, par excellence, we come to perceive the transcendent via the limitations of historical particularity. It is indeed true that the parables of the Good Samaritan, the Wedding Feast and the Prodigal Son, among many others, are full of psychological insight. It is also true, as McFague notes, that the western novel is haunted by the story of Jesus, since in so many stories we come to experience and recognise for ourselves that inexorable dichotomy between the temporal and the eternal. One of the characteristics of postmodernity is that it is supposed to have done away with any quest for a single, determinant 'truth'; yet so much contemporary fiction seems, paradoxically, obsessed precisely with such a search for 'answers', while those novels which remain perennially popular are those which attempt a serious engagement with universal questions. For example, the book which regularly tops readers' polls as the 'greatest English novel of the twentieth century' is J. R. R. Tolkien's decidedly old-fashioned fantasy story *The Lord of the Rings*, whose enduring popularity has been further underlined by its staggered release as a film trilogy, directed by Peter Jackson. Central to the novel is Tolkien's notion of what he called 'Recovery'. This is the remedy offered to what he saw, even in the 1940s and 50s, as the sickness of the world, so that things can be seen 'as we are (or were) meant to see them – as things apart from ourselves . . . so that the things seen clearly may be freed from the drab blur of triteness and familiarity – from possessiveness' ('On Fairy-stories', *Tree and Leaf*, pp. 58–9). Tolkien wrote against a background of war, possible invasion and defeat, and – in tune with the major issue of his time – was concerned about preserving the sorts of values to which political developments in Europe seemed so menacingly opposed. In Tolkien's saga, as R. J. Reilly (quoted by McFague) observes:

> We rediscover the meaning of heroism and friendship as we see the two hobbits clawing their way up Mount Doom; we see again the endless evil of greed and egotism in Gollum, stunted and ingrown out of moral shape by years of lust for the Ring; we recognize again the essential anguish of seeing beautiful and frail things – innocence, earthly love, children – passing away as we read of the Lady Galadriel and the elves making the inevitable journey to the West. (*Romantic Religion: A Study of Barfield, Lewis, Williams and Tolkien*, p. 206)

The themes of temptation, betrayal, providence, death, resurrection, courage and moral ambiguity are all present in Tolkien's epic. In reading about these themes we recognise their power and veracity because they are our themes too, and precisely those themes which in various forms we see reflected in our own struggles for meaning and coherence. It was those tendencies of his day towards greed, appropriation and avidity to which Tolkien was particularly opposed, and such tendencies have perhaps become even more marked in those contemporaneous manifestations of atomism, self-gratification and individualism which have been noted in earlier chapters. It is perhaps not so surprising, then, that *The Lord of the Rings* continues to resonate as a 'tract for the times' – and in the central symbol of the Ring, which becomes the focus of the twisted adoration and self-annihilation that is visited upon its wearers, we see an encapsulation of the darkest desires and deepest longings of the third millennium. Commenting perceptively on Tolkien's philosophy, Paul Kocher remarks that

> People and things are not meant to be our property; they belong to themselves. These are laws of our nature and theirs. The penalty for violation is a tormented exhaustion like Gollum's, a failure of perception like Sauron's, an exile from the healthy world of fact like the Ringwraiths'. Urging Bilbo to give up the Ring, Gandalf pleads 'Let it go! And then you can go yourself, and be free . . . Stop possessing it.' We are possessed, captured, by what we think we possess, says Tolkien. And if we believe we can wholly possess anything we delude ourselves. We, and Sauron, find our 'precious' slipping out of our fingers. Under our jaded eyes it turns into something different, which we no longer want; our appetite burns for fresh treasures, which we will discard in their turn. The people we master become denatured of their humanity; and the process of enslaving them denatures us. In this way, as in others, evil is self-defeating. A Sauron who succeeded in making himself tyrant over all of Middle-earth would only be the slave of the slave over whom he ruled. (*Master of Middle-Earth*, p. 62)

For Tolkien, liberation and transcendence come through self-denial, and it is in this process that the integrity of the self is made real. Since nobody who handles the Ring is able to evade the greed to possess it, which fastens on to him or her for ever afterwards, only a conscious moral decision to refuse it ensures complete immunity. This process of testing, of temptation, underscores the entire novel, and continually raises its dramatic stakes. Virtually every character of substance is put on trial: from Bilbo, who has the Ring to start with, through Gandalf, who vehemently refuses it, on to Aragorn, whose rejection of it endorses his worthiness to be king, and thence to Boromir, who covets the Ring and is killed, culminating in the magnificent renunciation by Galadriel. The queen of Lothlórien well knows that all the loveliness of the forest (fashioned by the power of Nenya, one of the three rings 'for the Elven kings under the sky') will fade upon the destruction of the One, ruling Ring, which is yet the only hope of the free world's salvation. In one of the great scenes of the novel she muses aloud on all that might be with the Ring's power at her disposal, and which is voluntarily offered her by Frodo (' "In place of the Dark Lord you will set up a Queen. And I shall not be dark, but beautiful and terrible as the Morning and the Night! Fair as the Sea and the Sun and the Snow upon the Mountain! Dreadful as the Storm and Lightning! Stronger than the foundations of the earth. All shall love me and despair!" '). But her true strength and power are revealed only as she shatters the dream herself: ' "I pass the test . . . I will diminish and go into the West, and remain Galadriel" ' (*The Lord of the Rings*, p. 385). Even Frodo, who at this mid-stage of the adventure still has the resilience and strength of will to contemplate giving up the Ring, later succumbs to its insidious power at the very Cracks of Mount Doom, wherein it is to be cast and unmade. He refuses to end the quest, proclaiming ' "I will not do this deed. The Ring is mine!" ', thereby using the very language of ownership that shows he is in fact now owned. Providence intervenes in the shape of Gollum, who bites off Frodo's ring-finger, loses his footing, and tumbles with the Ring into the furnace below. As Kocher observes, in Tolkien's universe 'the irony of evil is consummated by its doing the good which good could not do' (p. 47).

Fantasy-writing is fertile ground for theology and metaphysics, and has much to teach us. Arguably a more powerful treatment of self-abomination, excess and temptation even than that offered by Tolkien is to be found in the last novel of Ursula Le Guin's fine Earthsea trilogy, *The Farthest Shore*. The book might best be described as an extended, imaginative meditation on death, and on the necessity of the acceptance of death as the key to living authentically. All over Earthsea the joy, we are told, has gone out of life, while the efficacy of magic – the lifeblood of the inhabitants – is diminishing. (For our purposes, this might be read as a metaphor for the decline of traditional Christian religiosity.) Accordingly, the chief wizard – or Archmage – of Roke, who is named Ged, sets out on a journey to discover what the growing sickness infecting the land might be, and to try to put matters to rights. Ged takes with him a young prince from the island of Enlad, called Arren, of whom it has been prophesied that he will cross 'the dark land living and come to the far shores of the day'. The experiences of the pair on their quest reflect a number of the social ills blighting our own society. Stopping at Hort Town, one of the 'Seven Great Ports of the Archipelago', they find the city to be an evil and lawless place. Drug addicts sit in the market place and flies buzz around their lips; the goods sold are shoddy and sub-standard; thieves roam the streets; and despite the local colour, the atmosphere of the town seems sickly and unreal. Many adventures follow, during which Arren is sold into slavery, and rescued by Ged; Ged is wounded by hostile islanders, and almost dies; and Arren has nightmares full of his horror about death, counterpointed by a figure in his dreams who offers him immortality: 'There, in the vast, dry darkness, there one stood beckoning. Come, he said, the tall lord of shadows. In his hand he held a tiny flame no larger than a pearl, held it out to Arren, offering life. Slowly Arren took one step towards him, following' (*The Farthest Shore*, p. 63).

Finally the duo confront their enemy in the farthest west, on the island of Selidor. There a man by the name of Cob, who was formerly a mage (or 'man of power'), has worked a spell to enable him apparently to defeat death and move between the land of the dead and the living. Forced by his bodily destruction into the dark land, the land of the dead ('It was like a late twilight under clouds at the end of November, a dour, chill, dull air in which one could see, but not clearly and not far', p. 180), Cob is followed by Ged and Arren until they come to the source of the dry river, a gaping hole of nothingness, which we learn is the door Cob has opened between the worlds. This is a portal not only between death and life, but also in the minds of the living to that which they desire. The temptation that Cob offers is eternal life, but those who seek this path have appropriated living at the expense of life. They can no longer chant their songs, or work their spells, or do their craftsmanship well. Their lives no longer have meaning or fulfilment, and all in pursuit of an empty dream – without art, or love, or delight in work, life is lifeless. In a splendid passage, Le Guin presses home, through Ged, her own philosophy of the value of life and death:

> I will die . . . You will die . . . I prize that knowledge. It is a great gift. It is the gift of selfhood. For only that is ours which we are willing to lose. That selfhood, our torment and our glory, our humanity, does not endure. It changes and it goes, a wave on the sea. Would you have the sea grow still and the tides cease to save one wave, to save yourself? Would you give up the craft of your hands, and the passion of your heart, and the hunger of your mind, to buy safety? (p. 131)

Eventually Ged uses up his power ('all the skill of his life's training, and all the strength of his fierce heart') to close the door and make the world whole, but not before delivering a damning judgement on his adversary's creed of rapacious appropriation and self-absorbed cupidity:

> You exist, without name, without form. You cannot see the light of day; you cannot see the dark. You sold the green earth and the sun and the stars to save yourself. But you have no self. All that which you sold, that is yourself. You have given everything for nothing. And so now you seek to draw the world to you, all that light and life you lost, to fill up your nothingness. But it cannot be filled. Not all the songs of earth, not all the stars of heaven, could fill your emptiness. (p. 189)

This would be hard to better as a manifesto for a communitarian, socially engaged, and ecologically oriented mode of living, which runs counter to selfish individualism and corporate greed and acknowledges that the fragile beauty of life is bound up with responsibility for its upkeep. Nobody can have something for nothing. We are all going to die, but that's life, and the meaning of life is to be found not so much in a self-absorbed struggle to prolong it for its own sake as in the generous celebration and sharing of one's skills with others along the way. Le Guin's artistry here owes something to Taoism, but more perhaps to the poet Rilke, whose tenth Duino Elegy describes a town where the values are false because the inhabitants deny death and look only for distractions and satisfactions – a brilliant summary of our own present (see Barbara J. Bucknell, *Ursula K. Le Guin*, p. 56). However, beyond the town are the Laments, personified as women, who introduce those who have just died to their new land. They indicate the new stars above, and the mountains where pain was once quarried. At the foot of the mountains is a spring of joy, which among the living flows vigorously as a river. Le Guin knows the truth of Rilke's reflections on death: that death is part of life, and that denial of death, or a misguided attempt to appropriate life – or the lives of others – for unnatural or selfish ends, can lead only to disaster, and will exclude the capacity for true fulfilment. As Le Guin writes in another of her novels, 'Light is the left hand of darkness, and darkness the right hand of light. Two are one, life and death, lying together . . . like hands joined together, like the end and the way' (*The Left Hand of Darkness*, p. 199). Elsewhere Rilke describes death as 'The *side of life* that is turned away from us and not illuminated', in which 'we must try to achieve the greatest possible consciousness of our existence . . . at home in *both these unlimited realms*, and *inexhaustibly nourished by both*' (letter to Witold Hulewicz, 13 November 1925, *The Selected Poetry of Rainer Maria Rilke*, p. 316). This parallels both Le Guin and the end of his great elegy:

> But if the endlessly dead awakened a symbol in us,
> Perhaps they would point to the catkins hanging from the bare
> Branches of the hazel-trees, or
> Would evoke the raindrops that fall onto the dark earth in springtime. –
> And we, who have always thought
> Of happiness as *rising*, would feel

The emotion that almost overwhelms us
Whenever a happy thing *falls*.

(Rainer Maria Rilke, Tenth Elegy, *Duino Elegies*, ibid.)

What Tolkien called 'Recovery' is not confined just to the genre of fantasy, and a number of novels published in very recent years operate well within the mainstream of contemporary fiction. What these all have in common is an entirely secular operative framework and set of assumptions which are nevertheless profoundly offset by a capacity to explore metaphysical questions in an open-minded, sensitive, and often courageous manner. The best of these novels (and I will discuss two of these below) have nothing to do with urbanity or 'entertainment' (though they certainly do entertain), and everything to do with asking deep and painful questions about the meaning and end of human beings. Establishment Christianity often gets a rough ride, since for these writers the traditional conceptuality of the Christian tradition is no longer revelatory or authoritative. It has evolved, as Sallie McFague says, into 'tired clichés' and 'one-dimensional, univocal language' (*Speaking in Parables*, p. 23). The liberative message of the gospel needs to be rejuvenated and re-embodied, and in Colin Thubron's novel *Falling*, for example, this is most extraordinarily and movingly achieved.

*Falling* beautifully embodies that tension and finely attuned relationship between immanence and transcendence which is at the heart of human life and which is also the essence of Christian doctrine. Its central purpose is to explore metaphorically what it means to love at huge risk and maybe at great cost, and what it means to have love and life taken away. It deals with extremities of human experience and emotion, but entirely without sentiment, and feels all the more arresting in consequence. A young provincial journalist, Mark Swabey, is serving a short prison sentence for the manslaughter of his lover Clara, who was a trapeze artist in Appleby's Circus. The story opens with Swabey incarcerated and telling his story in flashback. He met Clara while reporting on the opening night of the circus at Peterhurst, the local town, for his newspaper, *The Hampshire*

*Times*. Captivated by her graceful and entirely unselfconscious performance on the high wire, which seems almost reverential to Mark ('she might have been beseeching somebody, or preparing to enter the darkness', p. 25), he visits her subsequently and falls in love with her. Swabey's relationship with Clara (whose circus name is 'The Swallow') is not without its complications, since he already has a girlfriend called Katherine, who is an artist in stained glass. One of the first of a series of dichotomies in the book, between earth and heaven, being and doing, thinking and acting, is explored by Thubron when he contrasts the two women in Mark's life. Katherine and Clara are quite different. Katherine is quiet, serious, middle class and – we are made to understand – is less passionate than compassionate. When Mark makes love to her he tells us that 'Beneath me she seemed physically to soften, as if in chemical change. She never achieved orgasm, and said she did not care. Loving to her was a kind of homecoming' (p. 11). Mark describes what he feels for her as some kind of 'recognition', as if Katherine were the 'sister whom my brother and I had invented in the nursery, to play tricks on' (ibid.). Clara, however, is all vivacious, energetic, powerful movement; uneducated and peripatetic, her self-sufficiency and passion for her art nevertheless give her 'a lodestar's separateness', eliciting in Mark 'a fervent disquiet' (p. 12). Mark describes her body 'as peculiarly her own', seeming 'not to flow, but to separate and bloom in its different parts, as if human flesh and blood were infinitely more complex than anyone had supposed' (p. 45).

Early in the book Katherine is commissioned to create a stained-glass window for a church depicting Lucifer's fall from heaven. Initially Mark feels that the composition is successful: 'In Lucifer Katherine had achieved a subtle triumph. In the end she had given him no colour at all, but had transformed his body in opalescent glass, frosted . . . by acid and soda crystals. Now, twisted in the slipstream of the leading, he divided paradise like an icicle, and plummeted to Hell in a white aureole of his own' (p. 58). Later, because he has actually experienced in Clara and her trapeze act that eternal moment when the soul strives for release from the body, and seeks the Other, he comes to see Katherine's art (which seems to derive more from the head than the heart) as reflecting the limitations of his own relationship with her: 'It was beautiful, of course, and in its way complete. But it struck me as stagnant now. It encompassed everything – sin, faith, damnation, paradise – yet related to nothing at all' (p. 62). Mark has been touched by something which is larger than him, has lived it for himself, and the substitutes are as emotionally insipid and drained of colour as Katherine's Lucifer.

Swabey is clearly heading for a choice not just between Katherine and Clara but between the different kinds of person he wants to be. Indeed, this is a novel that is profoundly concerned with choices and their consequences. Nominally he shares Katherine's values, and she is the kind of person who on the face of it would make a good choice of partner. Conversely, by the standards under which he has always operated, Clara would be entirely unsuitable. She is bound by birth and life to the circus, and has few possessions, which have to be cleared away every time the show moves on. Her life is entirely marginal and outside anything remotely approaching conventionality. However, finally none of this matters. Despite the risks, Mark realises 'with dulled astonishment' that he wants to marry her:

> The recognition came quite naturally, unbidden. With other women, with Katherine, the question of marriage had torn me with inner debate. But with Clara any decision was lifted out of my hands. I had no choice. Against this restful miracle, the fact that she was wedded to the circus, and that the circus excluded me, seemed unimportant. There would come a natural time for us, I thought. I would know the moment. (p. 68)

This existential decision made, a decision that the reader knows will have profound ramifications for Swabey at every level of his being, the novel moves into its final acts. At the point where his life has found its proper course, that moment of revelation where he has stumbled upon resolution – even though this will surely necessitate momentous life changes – Mark's world quite literally falls to earth, and apart. Clara, in attempting to go even higher on the trapeze, suffers an appalling fall when her forearm-brace snaps. She survives, but after several days in intensive care it is made clear to Mark that she is tetraplegic, and permanently paralysed from the neck down. Up to this moment every fibre of Clara's being has sought transcendence. Before her accident she dreams of her greatest ambition, and it is clear from what she says that she and her act, her identity and her art, are one. There is no separation: ' "I'd like to have my own troupe . . . and at the climax I'd leave the trapeze for a triple somersault. But I wouldn't want anyone to catch me. I'd just want to go on forever. Because that moment's not a preparation for any other moment. It's an end in itself. It's the real thing" ' (p. 81). Now her restless energy has been brought to nothing; like Lucifer she has fallen from the heavens, is reduced to a talking head, wracked with pain from damaged nerve-endings, and seems destined to die within months from renal failure. There now follows Mark's second great choice. He loves Clara, and even contemplates a life for the two of them together ('Home was a place I had invented for her now: a converted cottage with ramps and these breath-operated appliances. It would take time to adjust and automate, but it would be done', p. 120), but Clara is convinced that she wants to die:

> 'It's waking up that's worst. Everything's gone . . . There's not enough of me left. If it was you, there might be enough.' The tears were streaming down her cheeks. '*Please.*' She started to let out screaming gasps. '*Please.*'
>
> She shut her eyes tight against me, against the ceiling, everything.
>
> Just a head, weeping. (p. 132)

In an agony of his own, Mark succumbs to her wishes, and goes to France to buy barbiturates from a sympathetic chemist. At the last moment his courage almost fails him:

> I said: 'I can't do it.'

Then her voice broke in a faint, brittle sound which I still recognized as anger. 'Why do you want to keep me alive? Just so you can look at me? It's only because I'm helpless that I'm still alive. I don't want to go back in that place. I don't want to die alone. Or helpless like that.' Her fury burnt out into tears. 'Oh Mark, I'm sorry. I'm so sorry . . . Don't desert me now. You must understand.'

I said: 'I do.'

'Well, then?' Without her relief, her sudden peace, it would have been unendurable. I didn't want her last memory to be of my face as it was, so I went to a basin and dashed it over with a handkerchief. Then I sat quite calmly beside her. I even smiled. With every few capsules and sips of water, she said: 'Thank you, thank you,' afraid that I might stop. Then she was quiet in her pillows.

'I'll stay with you until you're sleeping.'

She said: 'It won't act before half an hour, will it? It's two hours before the nurse comes to turn me, but she's used to turning me in my sleep. They won't know.' She didn't realise that I would have to disconnect her respirator too, or it would gently keep her alive. After a while she said almost girlishly: 'Thank you. *Thank you*. It was good before this happened, it was wonderful.'

She asked me to rearrange her hands. For a while we exchanged our love, which was all of importance, and towards the end, as she became drowsy, she simply said: 'My arms are around you,' and I kissed her until she fell asleep.

And so I freed her into the dark. (pp. 136–7)

*Falling* is remarkable for its capacity to deal with the big issues with remarkable sensitivity and economy of style. It encompasses love, loss, courage, death, grief and finally acceptance within a mere 150 pages. In this respect, it is perhaps of all modern treatments of the high-wire business of living the most successful and authentic that I know. Like Clara the Swallow herself, it has complete integrity, because it refuses to pull its punches, flesh itself out, or pretend that life is anything other than immensely dangerous and precipitous. We can fall at any time. The rewards of living on the trapeze, of aiming and loving high, are immense; but the vulnerability and fragility that go hand in hand with such commitment are commensurate with the risk, and payback may never be far away. It is also, despite its secular setting, a profoundly theological novel. Religious imagery abounds, and it is deeply interested in the possibilities that may exist for human beings of transcendence and release from the mundane or superficial lives that constrain them. But like the parables, it knows that it is precisely in the ordinariness and even the banality of life that the transcendent is so often to be found. The miraculous may come upon us like a shaft of light from heaven, like a fallen angel. But that visitation is invariably ambiguous and unsettling. It is hard to be borne, and sometimes calls for the ultimate sacrifice.

As a result of Clara's death, Mark is imprisoned, and in jail – to his initial relief – he feels his entire identity fall away (images of ascent and descent recur throughout the novel). When the cell door shuts behind him, it closes 'less with a single clang than like the echo of many doors reverberating shut one after another; the noise seems to go on forever, as if every stage of your life were finding its definitive end' (p. 2). Prison regimen closes around his cauterised self, and the only real feelings that remain centre on the fact that 'she is not out there' (p. 3). Mark's face, we learn, 'has collapsed inward. Lines plough from the eyes' corners down to the jaw. The cheeks are gulleys, the eyes dead and glaring' (p. 3). He is in hell. Torment comes too in the form of the crass doctrinal orthodoxies of the prison chaplain, who seems to have little capacity for genuine warmth or empathy towards his charges. He and Swabey have a number of unsatisfactory interviews, when Mark becomes furious at the man's lack of understanding, and feels himself subjected only to platitudinous sermonising. Reflecting later on Swabey's case, the chaplain damns himself when he passes judgement on Clara:

> As far as I can judge, she was little more than a circus waif. Even her bravery on the trapeze suggests that of so many juveniles nowadays: the unconsidered rashness of youth, which thinks it will never die. These acrobatic feats are all

> very well, but the sceptic may reasonably enquire: to where was she ascending, and what for? (p. 139)

This sounds very much like clerical Everyman. One has the sense that Thubron has little but contempt for the liturgical post-office that the Church of England has become, as it dispenses vacuous pronouncements with no sense of the appropriateness or otherwise of their promulgation, or of their relevance to the challenges and ambiguities of real life. Thubron's own story of love and loss is itself the antidote: uplifting, demanding, truthful and generous-hearted, it speaks a thousand times more powerfully about the glory of living than could any credal formulation. And though Mark Swabey appears in the end bereft and without hope, he sees in the night-time escape of another prisoner, and 'lifer', Lorrimer, a recapitulation of the miracle of Clara's circus act: Lorrimer launches out over the perimeter wall on a cable, and in a simile that recalls the big top, is described as 'a giant sloth swinging into oblivion' (p. 149). Mark comes to understand in the end that, to paraphrase Alexander Blok, life is worth living only if you place exorbitant demands on it. Clara and Lorrimer belong to the same species, because they are fired by an inner conviction and integrity that goes way beyond sanitised notions of right and wrong, of conformity or nonconformity. Indeed, Lorrimer, like Clara, 'belongs somewhere else'. Unlike the other prisoners, Lorrimer 'burns with his self-belief, perched above some abyss of his own. The difference between him and them is more absolute than that between criminality and innocence' (p. 53). With great delicacy, Thubron appears to be implying that Mark has come to a new understanding – that Clara, whose soul blazed towards eternity in everything she was and did, has been released into a condition that coheres with her proper nature, and that on his own release from jail it might now be possible to return to the business of living.

Another novelist who does not shy away from extremity, and is all the more stimulating for that, is Hilary Mantel. Although her marvellous novel *A Change of Climate* is structured like a family saga, it has the thriller's power to shock. The central characters of the novel are a couple in early middle age, Ralph and Anna Eldred, to whom we are introduced as the parents of the young adults Katherine and Julian and of the younger children Robin and Rebecca. The family inhabit a rambling farmhouse in Norfolk. From here Ralph administers a charitable trust called Crucible House (loosely based, it seems, on Oxford House in Bethnal Green), which originated in philanthropic work among the poor of London's East End:

> It was to be an ambitious enterprise, with broad Christian interests: money for the missions, money for the East End doss house . . . Money above all for the deserving poor of Norfolk, the aged and indigent farm labourers, those churchgoing rural folk who had been mangled by agricultural machinery or otherwise suffered some disabling nuisance. (p. 50)

Over the years, the Eldreds' home has received on summer holiday, or simply for a period of recuperation, disturbed visitors from the city, tolerantly endured by Ralph's and Anna's children, and referred to by them either as 'Good Souls' or 'Sad Cases'. These desperately depressed urban refugees are offered rural sanctuary as part of the work of the trust. Ralph, it seems initially, is an energetic and conscientious man whose motivations are simply those of liberal Christian charity:

> He must see progress everywhere; he must see improvement. All day there must be action, or the simulation of it; letters in every direction, telephone calls, driving about the country and up and down to London; there must be advertising and exhortation, press campaigns and fund-raising drives. He took charge of policy, of the broader picture, engaged the services of a freelance public-relations expert; he rebuilt the hostel, updated its aims and methods. He granted an interview to the *Guardian* and one to *New Society* and was sometimes called into television studios to engage in futile scraps with those who thought differently about drugs, housing policy, education . . . He became well-known as one of those men who you telephone if you want something done; sometimes the novelty of his ideas outraged the *Eastern Daily Press*. The

> power of his will, he seemed to think, could pull the world into better shape. (pp. 253–4)

But this is a novel that Sallie McFague would recognise as thoroughly parabolic, in that we 'know' that something more is going on than appears on the surface to be the case, and that in all probability dramatic or distressing things are in store for us. Sure enough, Mantel soon informs us that Anna believes that, underneath everything, Ralph 'must know it is all an illusion. A futility' (p. 254). Like *Falling*, this novel is concerned fundamentally with loss, and with the moral choices contingent upon such loss. However, while Clara and Mark were young when disaster overtook them, Ralph and Anna by contrast have had many years to reflect on the catastrophe that engulfed them earlier in life, and to do their best to come to terms with the intolerable. Once again told in flashbacks, the story delivers its sting by degrees. It emerges that Anna and Ralph began their married life as missionaries. Acting on behalf of the trust, they went in the early days of the apartheid regime to South Africa, where they were required to make a stand on behalf of the African congregation of their township, Elim, against the discriminatory and oppressive policies of the Nationalist government. Acting with great moral courage, they were imprisoned and then deported from the country to a remote mission station in Bechuanaland (or modern Botswana), called Mosadinyana. In their new locale Anna, who by now is pregnant, gives birth to twins, named Matthew and Katherine. At this point, despite all the hardships they have endured, Ralph continues to believe that 'his choices have been the right ones, that this is where he wishes to be; believes it simply, as he believed in Bible stories when he was a child' (p. 235). But then the axe falls. Anna has fallen out with and dismissed Enock, a man prone to mysterious disappearances, who rakes the mission station garden, and is suspected of petty theft and drunkenness. One night, during a storm, Ralph is tricked into admitting Enock and his accomplices to the house. They take revenge for the slight Enock has suffered from Anna's insult by stabbing Ralph into unconsciousness and then abducting the twins. The next morning one twin, Katherine, is rescued alive from a ditch, making 'a jarring convulsive sound, louder and louder with each breath, as if her tiny ribcage were an uncoiling spring' (p. 241). The other child, Matthew, is never found. The police speculate that he has been taken alive to be dismembered piece by piece for medicinal body parts. Ralph records that 'one man said to me, "Sometimes we find traces." I asked him what he meant by traces, and he said, "substances, in bottles and jars" ' (p. 244). Later on, Ralph's sister Emma grieves for her brother's and sister-in-law's lost son in terms that underline the horror they have suffered:

> He would be six years old, he would be seven years old, he would be seventeen. He has all we lack, he is everything we are not; we have our gross appetites, but he is the opposite of flesh. Somewhere in Africa the little heart rots, the bird bones crumble or – alternatively – the traces dry in their jar; their child becomes a bush-ghost, powder on the wind. (p. 262)

Returning finally to England, the couple try to rebuild their shattered lives. But their Christian faith, their trust in rational, ordered goodness has gone. Ralph's uncle, James, suggests that they ask God for comfort, to which Anna retorts:

> 'It's impossible . . . I asked God for comfort when I came home to Elim every night, and saw these beaten people waiting for me on the stoep – but God kept very quiet, James. God did nothing. It was up to me to do something, but I acted within constraints – I tried to be good, you see, I felt the love of God biting into my wrists like a pair of handcuffs. So what did I offer these people? Bandages and platitudes. Suppose my training had been different? I might have stepped on the train to Cape Town with a revolver in my bag, I might have shot Dr Verwoerd – then I might have done some good in the world. Now, James – when I had in the room with me the man who was going to kill my child – when I had in my hand a broken bottle, suppose I had drawn the edges across his eyes? Suppose I had sliced his eyes to ribbons, suppose I had severed his veins and made him bleed

> to death? Then I would have done some good in the world.' (p. 247)

Gradually some semblance of normality returns, but after a time no reference is made to the loss of Matthew: 'Huge areas of reference were excluded by their family, their close friends. They were surrounded by acres laid waste, acres of silence' (p. 252). Always, though, the wound lies cold and malign at the heart of the Eldreds' marriage, draining its lifeblood, and eventually Ralph has an affair to escape from the grief and guilt he feels in Anna's company. The penultimate scene of the book, by which time Anna has discovered her husband's infidelity, depicts Ralph about to move out of their Norfolk home. Reconciliation seems impossible, and this act of betrayal for the one, and of solace for the other, appears to have crushed any prospect of the past's resolution in favour of the present. Yet despite all their shared pain, or perhaps because of it, neither wants to endure final separation, even though events seem to have acquired their own momentum. Ralph is actually picking up his suitcases to leave, when – in an extraordinarily dramatic finale – one of the trust's summer visitors, a drug addict called Melanie (who has run away first from Anna, and then from the hospital where she has been incarcerated after overdosing), crawls towards them in a tableau that recapitulates the surviving twin Katherine's retrieval from an African ditch:

> A creature moved into their view, at a distance. It came slowly over the rough ground, crawling. It was a human being: its face a mask of despair, its body half clothed in a flapping gown, its hands and knees and feet bleeding; its strange head the colour of the sun. It progressed towards them; they saw the heaving ribs, the small transparent features, the dirt-ingrained skin.
>
> 'I must put these cases down somewhere,' Ralph said. All he could think for the moment was that they were dragging his arms out of his sockets; he did not know whether to put them inside or outside the house. He wondered which of them would move first, he or Anna, toward this jetsam, this

> salvage; but wondered it idly, without that spirit of competition in goodness that had animated his life. Whichever, it didn't matter . . . He put his baggage down, nowhere in particular, wedged across the threshold. 'We must take her in,' he said to Anna. 'Or she will die.'
>
> 'Yes,' Anna's face was open, astonished. They left the Red House together, stumbling over the rough grass. As they approached the child, she stopped trying to crawl. She shrank into herself, her head sunk between her shoulder blades like some dying animal. But then, as they reached out towards her, Melanie began to breathe – painfully, slowly, deeply, sucking in the air – as if breathing were something she were learning, as if she had taken a class in it, and been taught how to get it right. (p. 340)

In Melanie's distress the Eldreds are able to reassert their common bond, and reconcile their dreadful past loss into present assistance, without artifice or forced philanthropy, for a human being who simply needs their immediate help. In this act of selfless – as distinct from forced or willed – charity, the earlier act of rescuing Katherine is reaffirmed and simultaneously neutralised as the inescapable obverse of her twin's murder. By accepting Melanie without preconditions, Ralph and Anna are also able to find some measure of acceptance, of themselves, of each other, and of what has happened to them both. In the book's closing scene, Emma, Ralph's sister, returns to the Walsingham church that she visits at the novel's outset, and adds the name of Matthew to the line she had earlier left blank. Thereby she completes the list of the Eldred family to be prayed for at the shrine, while at the same time reintegrating Matthew's memory into public consciousness and signalling the family's reunion. The 'change of climate' of the title thus refers both to the Eldreds' reversion from Africa to England, and to the shift in their moral and spiritual compass at the book's end. It also describes the dichotomy between an inexplicable and evil act and a measurably good one, and the ramifications for good or ill that result in each instance. At one point in the novel Ralph compares his and Anna's tragedy to a stain which always returns, 'like the blood in Bluebeard's room': 'He understood, then, what the fairy-tale means; blood is never wiped out. No bad action goes away. Evil is energy, and perpetuates itself; only its form changes' (p. 253). In spite of the odds against it, and without taking anything away from all the horror and pain that follow from the suspension of moral conscience, Mantel is able – in the end convincingly – to assert, contrary to Ralph's analogy, that the nullification of evil is a real possibility, as are acceptance and forgiveness. Transformation may thus be substantive rather than just of form.

Neither *Falling* nor *A Change of Climate* are in any respect 'comfortable' novels. They tackle immense – and immensely difficult – themes, and attempt to make sense of the largely senseless. What is remarkable about them is that their creators, who are both secular writers, have managed to fashion from their materials stories that move and touch us deeply at the level of our own experience. While rejecting false pieties and the consolations of impoverished doctrine, Mantel and Thubron nevertheless revel in theological storytelling, and succeed thereby in constructing for us new temples for our thoughts, our prayers and aspirations. These are transcendent novels, even while they are rooted in the here and now, because they look beyond themselves to a place where, despite all the pain which went before, there is yet the possibility of reconciliation, resolution and hope. Nothing is taken away from the agony of the journey to Calvary, or of the weight and burden of the cross, because these writers know well that it would be wrong to do so. Their integrity as writers emerges because they do not hide from us what we know to be true, that life is terribly hard. Their further stature lies in the fact that they also show us that that struggle is not all that there is.

# CHAPTER 6

# Resources for a Secular Theology (2): Film

If access to the divine is to be had in secular life, perhaps it is in the cinema that people most closely approach communion. In cinemas and movie theatres people come together in a sense of expectation and shared purpose, and they come to be uplifted, educated, involved, moved, or simply to be entertained. They can discover wisdom, insight and moral purpose on celluloid, the most 'popular' and – despite its links to big business – genuinely democratic cultural medium, apart perhaps from television, that there is. Cinema emphatically reminds us of the importance of a public dimension to any credible Christian theology. Moreover, since all of life is a process of storytelling, a recounting of our own lives and the effect our lives have on other lives, and on the world around us, it comes as no surprise that the visual power and narrative immediacy of film is seen to capture our stories so richly and powerfully. But perhaps film also captures something else altogether – some communication of a world that comes to us from without, mediated in often ambiguous and mysterious ways.

Nick Willing's fine film *Photographing Fairies* (1997) explores this idea metaphorically: the elusive and dangerous fairies, who indirectly precipitate a string of disasters in the lives of the film's protagonists, come to be seen as 'God's messengers', heralds from another realm. Their existence can be proven and recorded only through the single-exposure shots of a professional photographer, Charles Castle. Castle, who has lost his wife (to whom he was married for only a single day) in a mountaineering accident, comes to believe that the fairies have been sent to tell him that he will be reunited with her in another world, which is actually 'but a footfall away'. These dark or homeless angels are duly captured on celluloid, and the photographic 'proof' which the formerly sceptical Castle secures of their existence is enough to convince him to join his wife precipitately in death. The final shot of the film shows Castle and his wife caught in apparently the same alpine blizzard as that in which she let go his hand and slid into a crevasse; except this time, in the life beyond, Castle has the strength to pull her out, and now towards a different order of salvation.

The idea that the transcendent may be 'captured' on film is attracting much attention, as the number of recent articles and books on theology and cinema indicates. One writer in a representative collection entitled *Explorations in Theology and Film* summarises an emerging consensus when he observes that 'The narrative of film can function either as a subversive story which rethinks the religious tradition (like the parables), or it can even become an alternative religious narrative which reinterprets reality in a new way' (David John Graham, 'The Uses of Film in Theology', p. 42). There is a growing sense that film is actually *good* for theology, in that it allows the Christian tradition to be mediated in exciting and creative new ways. The subject is even beginning to receive attention from conservative writers, who might previously have been expected to treat the medium with suspicion. For example, the evangelical scholar Robert K. Johnston writes in a recent book that

> God is present in all of life and communicates with us through all of these theological resources. Film, as an expression of the broader culture and as the occasion for our own personal experiences and growth, can serve as a theological resource, providing both insight and conviction to its viewers. For when the dialogue comes together between a viewer and a film, one may glimpse something hidden, either in one's self, another, or even the Other. (*Reel Spirituality*, p. 85)

Perhaps it is in a number of science fiction films that we see our present preoccupations most truthfully reflected. Accordingly, it is perhaps also in that genre that we see portrayed some of the most significant representations of a religious and theological sensibility. Science fiction, once described by the novelist Ian McEwan as 'the only subject left worth writing about', frequently shows in graphic and prophetic terms the consequences of capitalism's excesses, as well as many of the damaging extremities of postmodernity. Science fiction, in creating new spaces, frontiers and dimensions, holds up a mirror to ourselves and our world, and indicates a range of possibilities. Much of the power of its vision consists in the fact that the theology which emerges is usually implicit, and is translated into terms which are culturally palatable and open to empathy. The utopian aspirations of modernism have little place here; it is rather dystopian worlds and universes which predominate. Frequently – as in the films *Alien* (1979) and *Blade Runner* (1982) – they critique corporate capitalism while also redefining our understandings of the nature of human being. For example, *Blade Runner* – Ridley Scott's visual feast of dark, rain-washed alleys and sidewalks – directly addresses the dangers, confusions and disorientations of life in the postmodern city, where not just one's priorities but even one's whole sense of identity may ultimately be at risk.

*Blade Runner,* which was adapted from an influential novel by Philip K. Dick called *Do Androids Dream of Electric Sheep?* (1968), has come to be seen as the prime cinematic exemplar of the postmodern, in that it takes up some of the key themes identified by the 'inventor' of postmodernism, Fredric Jameson, in his seminal book *Postmodernism*. Jameson drew attention here to the emergence of cyberpunk, a sub-genre of science fiction (taking its name from ideas discussed in William Gibson's novel *Neuromancer,* 1984) which *Blade Runner* directly influenced and helped to define. For one commentator such attention on Jameson's part reveals an important truth: that science fiction has, in many ways, actually 'prefigured the dominant issues of postmodern culture' (Scott Bukatman, *Blade Runner*, p. 48). Bukatman writes that

> Cyberpunk, like the *film noir* from which it was partly derived,

> was defined as much by its tone and attitude as by its icons and narrative structures. Its high-tech urban settings were congested and confusing, yet also exhilarating. Communications and information media defined its future, and information density defined its style. *Blade Runner*'s cyberpunk urbanism exaggerates the presence of the mass media, evoking sensations of unreality and pervasive spectacle: advertising 'blimps' cruise above the buildings . . . and gigantic vid-screens dominate the landscape with images of pill-popping geishas. (p. 49)

The Los Angeles of Ridley Scott is a city in which life has little solidity and few firm footholds. In the year 2019, much of the city's populace has abandoned earth for the 'off-world colonies', leaving behind the unwilling, the unfit, or the otherwise discriminated against. This metropolis of the future is drenched in rain and fog, while huge refineries belch fire and smoke into an ominous and polluted sky. Into this inferno descend several fugitive androids, or 'replicants'. Though they are forbidden to return to earth on pain of death, they have come nevertheless to seek an extension of their four-year life-span by confronting their 'maker', Dr Eldon Tyrell (the instigator of the android – or 'Nexus 6' – production line), and forcing him to alter their genetic make-up. Assigned to track them down is the eponymous blade runner (or state-condoned bounty hunter) of the film's title, Rick Deckard (played by Harrison Ford). In his search for the androids he is confronted by a still more worrying quest, that of holding on to a coherent sense of his own identity in the midst of danger and disjuncture. Deckard's turns out to be a bumpy ride. Contravening his professional code, since blade runners are supposed to be without feelings, Deckard kills two of the female replicants in edgy panic (by shooting them in the back), then simultaneously falls in love with a fifth replicant, Rachael, who is an employee of the Tyrell Corporation. He is almost killed, first by the android Leon (and is only saved at the last gasp by Rachael, who shoots Leon in the head), and then by the fourth replicant, the leader of the band, Roy Batty (brilliantly and chillingly played by Rutger Hauer), with whom Deckard fights desperately for his life at the film's denouement. During the course of his purgatorial adventures, in which Deckard barely hangs on as he is beaten up, strangled, and then has his fingers broken by the physically superior and much stronger androids, it is even implied that he may himself be a replicant. Little wonder, then, that the viewer's own sense of orientation – which at the start of the movie relates sympathetically to Deckard's apparent status as 'hero', but is by the end unbalanced by his transition to something much more ambivalent – finds itself challenged by the multiple ambiguities presented by the film. The boundaries between human beings and replicants are continually blurred, threatening to undermine the fundamental distinction between human and machine. This is an entirely postmodern phenomenon, where, in Bukatman's words, 'Nothing can any longer distinguish between sign and referent, simulation and original – and anyway, there is no longer any reason to make the distinction' (p. 69).

The postmodern aesthetics of the film may be further discerned in the way that it mixes up its sense of time. In their book *Science Fiction Cinema: From Outerspace to Cyberspace*, Geoff King and Tanya Krzwinska note that *Blade Runner* is meant to be set in the future, but that a central ingredient of its visual effectiveness is the look and feel of 1940s *film noir*: 'The future is not imagined as bright, gleaming or progressive, but as something that has ingrown or turned back on itself. This, again, is the kind of thing said to characterise the postmodern: a loss of clear historical perspective, a juxtaposition of detail from different periods' (p. 55).

Further ambiguities arise in the film's treatment of memory. Replicants are enabled to function in the world because they are genetically programmed with other people's memories, memories reinforced by the provision of faked photographs; and it is its exploration of memory which provokes some of the film's most profound metaphysical reflections. Although memories are sometimes equated with identity, *Blade Runner* makes it clear that this is a dangerous practice. Even for humans, memories are not givens, as Bukatman notes, but are selected, distorted and misremembered: 'Our pasts are, to some extent, constructions; so then are ourselves' (p. 79). While the gorgeous surface visuals of *Blade Runner* mesmerise and seduce the viewer, the images actually *within* the film can be treacherous:

> The inescapable photographs that show up throughout *Blade Runner* are constantly being handled and flipped over, which emphasises their equally inescapable flatness and depthlessness. Memories are no more indelible than the paper a photograph is printed on; history is devalued as a guarantor of truth, stability and unified meaning. Photographs are constantly evoked as signs, but they are ultimately empty signs, signifiers of nothing. (Bukatman, p. 80)

Yet despite the miasma of signs detected by many of those who have written about it, it seems to me that the film does maintain a certain integrity in its portrayal of the quest for ultimate meaning and hope (even if it does not also indicate a route to the procurement of easy answers). After their climactic battle on the rooftops of the Bradbury Building, Deckard is finally rescued by Batty from certain death when he is unexpectedly hauled by his adversary away from the roof's edge and the dizzying drop below. Roy releases a dove into the ether, a symbol of reconciliation (or the Holy Spirit), then sits down with his opponent and tells him that 'I've seen . . . things you people wouldn't believe. Attack ships on fire off the shoulder of Orion. I've watched C-beams glitter in the dark near the Tannhauser Gate. All those moments will be lost, in time. Like tears in the rain . . . Time to die.' Batty's limited allocation of time – his four-year life-span – has finally run out, prompting Deckard's voice-over (in the original cut of the film) to enquire: 'I don't know why he saved my life. Maybe in those last moments he loved life more than he ever had before. Not just his life. Anybody's life. My life. All he'd wanted were the same answers the rest of us want. Where did I come from? Where am I going? How long have I got? All I could do was sit there and watch him die.' Despite their titanic struggle, and the death of Roy's companions (including his android lover Pris) at Deckard's hands, and all the ambiguity about Deckard's own status as human/replicant,

Roy is able lyrically to affirm the veracity and value of his own memories ('real', not manufactured) as well as hold out a bond of, ironically enough, common humanity and mortality to his erstwhile foe. Although he has, by his own admission, done 'questionable things' (including the murder of Tyrell), Roy emerges in the end as a profoundly sympathetic figure, whose chief motivation is simply to understand who and what he is and what his death amounts to. This universal search is one to which we can all relate. In the course of his own quest, which mirrors that of Deckard, Batty is imbued with metaphysical significance. After killing Tyrell, he rides the elevator back down the side of the corporation pyramid, gazing heavenward in the only frame in the film where there are stars to be seen: 'And they're moving away from him, as if he's some kind of fallen angel' (Bukatman, quoting Hampton Fancher in Paul Sammon's *Future Noir: The Making of Blade Runner*, p. 178). Later on, in order to prolong his life by a few moments more, so that reconciliation with Deckard may be achieved, Batty drives a nail into the palm of his hand, the agony of which keeps him going beyond his appointed time: 'Time . . . enough,' he breathes. The Christian overtones are by now explicit, reinforced by the flight of the dove (which brings to mind Psalm 54:6: 'And I said, Oh that I had wings like a dove, so that I might fly away and find rest'). After Roy's death, Deckard maintains the metaphysical and reflective tone, and muses, upon returning to his apartment and finding his own replicant lover Rachael unharmed by the police, 'I didn't know how long we'd have together. Who does?'

Life and identity in the postmodern city are attractive subjects for current filmmakers, especially when these topics can be read through the 'grid' of science fiction. Similar takes on these themes are visible in films such as Luc Besson's *The Fifth Element* (1997), Alex Proyas' *Dark City* (1997), Terry Gilliam's *Brazil* (1984), and *The Matrix* (1999), directed by the Wachowski brothers. A recurring component of such films tends to be their use of dialectical oppositions, which include: spirituality versus materialism; ruthless corporatism versus offbeat individuality or collectivism; and science/technology versus faith. These binary oppositions, like the human/android dialectic discussed above, invariably articulate distinctively postmodern – and therefore thoroughly contemporary – anxieties.

*The Matrix* and *The Fifth Element* both construct worlds where messianic figures come to the rescue of a humanity under siege. *The Matrix* owes much to the sort of cyberpunk pioneered by *Blade Runner.* Although initially a term used to describe William Gibson's writing, cyberpunk is now more generally understood to refer to that sub-genre of science fiction which is, as King and Krzwinska define it, 'characterised by sub-cultural use of computers and other types of technology, such as neuro-implants, which permit physical interaction with the digital world' (p. 115). Indeed, the city in which the action takes place in the film is nothing more or less than a construction run from a master computer program. Thomas Anderson, who goes by the hacker alias Neo, and is a supplier of pirate programs, is contacted by a group of VR resistance fighters, led by the mysterious Morpheus and backed up principally by his lieutenant Trinity, both of whom have extraordinary, almost God-like, reputations among hackers. This group persuade Neo that what he believes to be life in 1999 is in fact a simulation projected by hostile forms of artificial intelligence existing in, or close to, 2199. The latter's program is called the Matrix. For Graham Ward, the messianism of the film is clear:

> Neo is the one Morpheus has been looking for to save the city which is tantamount to saving the real as distinct from the virtual. The real is encoded in another framework called Zion. Neo incarnates this programme, which is superior finally to the Matrix. But we only come to understand this, as Neo comes to understand his own mission, by returning to the cyber city, now intellectually trained (through various computer-generated simulations) in a battery of Japanese martial arts skills. In a visit to the Oracle (who can determine whether Neo is the One), Morpheus is captured. In a logic of sacrifice-as-gift (a Judaeo-Christian logic), Morpheus surrenders his life to the agents of the Matrix within the cyber city. Neo rescues him and reveals that he is programmed from a different framework than the Matrix, a more powerful

> and, seemingly, more humane and transcendent framework, draped in Judaeo-Christian imagery, shot through with Buddhist spirituality and a Hellenic paganism . . . In the last scene, which follows the resurrection of Neo from the dead by the love of Trinity . . . Neo sends a message to the Matrix which signals the failure of its system. (*Cities of God*, p. 242)

For Ward the film is a 'visual multimedia extravaganza' (p. 243), but one which, since the cyber city remains in the end in place, does not break free of its own power games. Be that as it may, *The Matrix* does truthfully articulate an intense anxiety about our increasing domination by the tools of AI. Although they were devised to make human communication more efficient and straightforward, these have actually enslaved people to reams of e-mails (much of it junk) and consigned them to desk-bound isolationism. The idea that we are in thrall to a faceless network of computer programs running our lives is one that would find common currency among legions of harassed office workers, while the further notion that 'altering the program' (infecting the whole system with a virus, perhaps?) can bring about liberation from slavery to the virtual might be found highly attractive in many quarters. *The Matrix*'s themes would be likely to chime too both with civil rights activists campaigning for greater freedom of information (with their strong misgivings about the secrecy of government and the misuse of personal data for corporate ends), and with anti-globalisation campaigners and NGOs (who discern in western democracies precisely the kind of ruthless self-interest and corporate power evinced by the 'sentient life-forms' of the film).

A less complex but no less malevolent kind of enemy is portrayed in *The Fifth Element*. Every five thousand years a vast field of evil energy bursts into our universe and attempts to exterminate all life. The only thing that can combat it is the long-lost ultimate weapon, the Fifth Element. The Fifth Element itself proves to be not a doomsday device but, as Andrew Harrison rather frivolously but accurately puts it, 'Milla Jovovich's beautiful humanoid girl, Leeloo, with enhanced DNA, orange hair and a voice half way between Björk and that bird-kid from the G-Force cartoons' ('New Adventures in Sci-Fi', *Neon*). Jovovich as the Fifth Element is guided towards safe despatch of her mission through the heroics of taxi-driver Korben Dallas (Bruce Willis), and a priest called Cornelius (Ian Holm) who is the guardian of the stones – representing the four elements of earth, air, fire and water – without which Jovovich cannot complete her task and annihilate evil. The messianism of Besson's film is of an entirely less sophisticated kind than that visualised in *The Matrix*. Nevertheless, the idea that the world can be 'saved' via the intervention of a cosmic super-being in human form is explicitly Christian: even though Besson's super-being, in a rather idiosyncratic personal touch, emerges as a six-foot Russian model speaking 'the ancient language' of the stars (unintelligible to everybody except Ian Holm) with a somewhat dubious – though altogether contemporary! – holistic connectedness to pyramids, ancient stones and inner harmony. However, the film has its serious side, and in its condemnation of war and violence, as well as its juxtaposition of Leeloo's bodily 'perfection' against the screaming, ceaseless noise and confusion of the city (23rd-century Manhattan), a number of the perennial anxieties of postmodernity are authentically and entertainingly addressed.

One of the most creative examinations of the prevalence of theological themes in film has been provided by Gerard Loughlin, who in a number of recent articles and his book *Alien Sex: The Body and Desire in Cinema and Theology* offers a perceptive discussion of cinematic notions of sexuality, corporeality and transcendence. In discussing the movies *Alien*$^3$ (1992) and *Se7en* (1995), Loughlin notes that

> One might think of David Fincher's films as neo-medieval texts, not just because *Alien*$^3$ dresses its prisoners in monk-like garb and alludes to Augustine, while *Seven* refers to Aquinas and Dante, but because both films concentrate on a central medieval concern: the decrepitude and corruption of the body. The camera lingers on rotting, gouged or otherwise mutilated flesh, or, in startling close-ups, shows us body-parts variously invaded or caressed. These films look with a certain

> tenderness on the perishability and defeat of the body: on the presence of death in life. ('Ending Sex', *Sex These Days*, p. 206)

For Loughlin, *Alien*[3] in particular is 'replete with religious resonance' (p. 212), where the story of Ripley's fall to the penal planet Fiorina – or Fury – 161 in an escape craft (or descent into hell), can 'be read as a horribly inverted Christian nativity play, with Ripley taking the part of the Virgin Mary'. Ripley (Sigourney Weaver) arrives among the prisoners on Fury (who have taken a vow of celibacy) as Eve the temptress, but also as the second Eve, bearing their nemesis – the alien queen – within her body. Ripley's conception has preserved her virginity (her child was conceived by an alien being among the stars, and has no human father), and will bring to the inhabitants of Fury redemption through heroic and desperate struggle with the monster: as Loughlin puts it, 'a parody of the Christian hope of life through death with Christ' (p. 212). Loughlin convincingly interprets these themes in terms of contemporary anxieties about the body and risk of its infection (for example with the HIV virus); sexual identity; death; and, within society, increasingly ambiguous gender roles and expectations.

Arguably it is in the films of the Russian filmmaker Andrei Tarkovsky (1932–86) that cinema has most closely captured a sense of direct access to the religious and the transcendent, especially in his widely admired science fiction films *Solaris* (1972) and *Stalker* (1979). Although he is often regarded as something of an 'art house' director, interest in Tarkovsky is growing; furthermore, in the Soviet Union he was a controversial figure, to the degree that on its eventual release in 1971 his second film *Andrei Rublev* (1966) played to sell-out audiences. Although his films certainly are dense, richly textured and provocative, it would be wrong, I believe, to think of him as rarefied or obscure. Indeed, his central interests are always clear. Tarkovsky was concerned in all his work with the travails of a world caught between the ignorance and stupidity of uncontrolled technological 'progress' and its consequent loss of reverence, spirituality and 'faith'. He viewed his role as a filmmaker and artist in strongly ethical and moral terms, and throughout his own book on the cinema wrote consistently about art in language strongly appropriate to religion; for example: 'In art, as in religion, intuition is tantamount to conviction, to faith' (*Sculpting in Time*, p. 41). His book actually ends with these words: 'Perhaps the meaning of all human activity lies in our artistic consciousness, in the pointless and selfless creative act? Perhaps our capacity to create is evidence that we ourselves were created in the image and likeness of God?' (pp. 241–2). Given these fundamental convictions, it is not surprising that all of Tarkovsky's films are chock-full with theological images, themes and questions. However, one of the reasons that I view him as such an important figure is that he was by no means dogmatic or prescriptive about religion. His belief in God was complemented by an interest in literature, eastern music and philosophy, astrology, Buddhism, and Taoism. He was profoundly interested in how different modes of culture could reconcile life and faith. In this respect, he seems to be a paragon of the kind of creative theological reflection for which I'm calling in this book.

In his third film, *Solaris*, Tarkovsky chose to turn to science fiction by adapting a novel of the same name by the Polish writer Stanislaw Lem. Tarkovsky kept hold of the essential outline of Lem's story, as well as much of the dialogue. However, his eventual interpretation of it was very different from Lem's own, much to the novelist's indignation at the time. In Tarkovsky's version, the astronaut Kris Kelvin (Donatas Banionis) travels to a space station orbiting the mysterious planet Solaris to make contact with the station's existing personnel, the scientists Gibarian, Sartorius and Snaut, and determine whether the research being conducted there should be concluded and the station closed down. The subject of the research is the planet itself, which manifests a number of strange and disturbing characteristics that have profoundly affected previous astronauts and research teams – some have disappeared, and others have seemingly suffered weird hallucinations. On Kelvin's arrival he finds that Gibarian, the leader of the expedition, is dead, while the remaining members of the team, Snaut and Sartorius, appear furtive and preoccupied. Kelvin comes to realise that, having been subjected to illegal doses of radiation from the station, the planet in return has somehow extracted memories from the scientists and brought into being 'visitors' from their various pasts, who now walk the research station as replicas or simulacra of the people back on earth on whom they are modelled. It was through coming into contact with his visitor that Gibarian decided to take his own life, apparently out of 'shame'. Collapsing exhausted in his quarters, after his long journey and the shock of encountering phenomena that he cannot explain or understand, Kelvin wakes to find that he has been joined by his long-dead wife, Hari (Natalya Bondarchuk), who committed suicide ten years before as a direct result (it seems) of his neglect. Although Hari, like the androids in *Blade Runner* (and here in an even more exact sense), is a 'replicant', Kelvin comes to see that through her, and their love, he may achieve reconciliation with all those whom he has betrayed or let down in the past. In this sense he is 'redeemed' from the cold, scientific and rationalistic outlook that has been his disposition before, and attains a new kind of self-awareness which is profoundly bound up with a connectedness to humanity, the earth, and its wonders.

For Lem (a writer of 'hard' science fiction) the love story of Kris Kelvin's reunion with his dead wife Hari (or Rheya in the book) is fundamentally a device through which he can explore what occurs when human beings 'try to stay human in an inhuman situation' (*Solaris*, p. 147). There is a glimpse of hope at the end of the book, when, after Rheya's final disappearance, Kelvin, against all evidence and reason, looks towards a possibility that 'the time of cruel miracles was not past' (p. 195). Apart from this, the chief theme is 'Kris's realisation that the human values we cherish, such as love, have no significance or meaning in a universe that is probably organised along principles that we can never even begin to understand' (Vida T. Johnson and Graham Petrie, *The Films of Andrei Tarkovsky*, p. 102). This unaccommodating rationalistic framework was uncompromisingly rejected by Tarkovsky, who transformed Lem's story into an affirmation of human values and the power of love in an indifferent or menacing universe. The central figure in this reinterpretation is Hari, who as Johnson and Petrie remark is 'perhaps more fully a human being than the coldly detached

Sartorius, who tells her cruelly that she is just a mechanical copy of the "real" Hari' (p. 103). Hari, who tells the men that she and the other visitors are 'yourselves, your conscience', shows a true capacity to love. In the end, since she knows that her continuing existence is contingent only on her proximity to Solaris (and that for as long as she is alive she and Kris are doomed to live forever on the station) she sacrifices herself by undergoing voluntary disintegration in a particle annihilator constructed by Sartorius. In between, unable to reconcile her love for Kris and the despair she feels at their predicament, Hari attempts to kill herself by drinking liquid oxygen. However, since her bodily composition is not human (and is made up not of atoms, but of neutrinos) she is miraculously resurrected. As well as being more profoundly human than some of the humans, Hari is thus an otherworldly and redemptive figure who incarnates in her person the possibility of both literal and moral transformation, consummately expressed in her final sacrifice. Johnson and Petrie note that 'In Hari's first two appearances, the gravity and serenity of her behaviour, combined with lighting that bathes her in a golden glow and frames her, shawl outspread, against the brightness of the porthole, barely needs support from words or actions in establishing the essence of what she represents in the film' (p. 110).

Tarkovsky's hostility to scientific rationalism, and to technological development without an accompanying morality (epitomised in *Solaris* by self-interested exploitation of the planet and in Sartorius' callous response to the consequences), is pressed home with equal vigour and aesthetic sensibility in his next film, *Stalker.* As I have noted in Chapter 2, Tarkovsky adapted his story from the novel *Roadside Picnic* by the Strugatsky brothers, whose content is summarised on pages 32–3. Once again, although Tarkovsky retained the essential outlines of the original story, and although the Strugatskys were themselves hired to write the film script, it is clear that the director altered the main themes significantly, in order to make the film much more substantially 'Tarkovskian'. Johnson and Petrie cite the Strugatskys telling the audience at the film's premiere not to believe the credits: 'We are not the scriptwriters, he did it all –

alone' (p. 138). Rather like Lem, the Strugatskys are interested in their novel in questions of knowledge and interpretation: if the zones are indeed the result of alien visitation, what was the aliens' purpose? What is the meaning of Red's sacrifice of Arthur in order to save his own daughter? But these questions are virtually passed over by Tarkovsky, who turns the science fiction framework into something intensely personal and acutely probing of the human condition. There is only one zone in the film, and the characters who, for their various reasons, enter it are all changed: Stalker is far more sympathetic than the Red in the book, and appears to signify faith and belief; Professor, like Sartorius, seems to represent rationalist materialism; and Writer appears to incarnate a creative capacity that has warped into cynical, self-absorbed egotism. Tarkovsky himself described the film as being 'about the existence of God in man, and about the death of spirituality as a result of our possessing false knowledge' (*Sculpting in Time*, p. 159); and the film's main objective would indeed seem to be to provide a commentary on a world 'dominated by transitory material concerns, in which faith and spirituality have been forgotten or discarded' (Johnson and Petrie, p. 145). Slavoj Žižek certainly regarded *Stalker*, because of what he interpreted as its clear and powerful critique of consumption and materialism, as Tarkovsky's finest film:

> In . . . evergrowing piles of inert, dysfunctional 'stuff', which cannot but strike us with their useless, inert presence, one can, as it were, perceive the capitalist drive at rest. That is the interest of Andrei Tarkovsky's films, most vividly his masterpiece *Stalker*, with its post-industrial wasteland: wild vegetation overgrowing abandoned factories, concrete tunnels and railroads full of stale water and wild undergrowth in which stray cats and dogs wander . . . The ultimate irony of history is that it was a director from the Communist East who displayed the greatest sensitivity to this obverse of the drive to produce and consume. (*The Fragile Absolute*, p. 41)

Undergirding this critique is a framework of biblical reference and Christian iconography, which is most clearly evident in the scene frequently referred to as 'Stalker's Dream', when the men – Writer, Professor and Stalker himself – rest before entering the 'Meatgrinder':

> They are seen in a series of individual shots, with Writer lying prone on a mossy patch of earth projecting into a stream; Professor half sitting, half lying on a slope; and Stalker lying full-face, facing in the opposite screen direction to Writer, almost entirely surrounded by water, with a waterfall visible behind him. After a brief cut – to what looks like quicksand and a background of trees, with windspouts and the unmotivated fluff that usually signals 'strangeness' – an off-screen woman's voice (probably Stalker's wife) begins to whisper the passage from Revelation 6:12–17 about the opening of the sixth seal, the destruction of Heaven and Earth, and the vain attempts by the survivors to hide themselves from 'the wrath of the Lamb'. A brief shot of Stalker in close-up is followed by a cut to black and white and another extreme close-up of his sleeve and then his face before the camera tracks away . . . over a collection of debris lying in shallow water: a syringe, a bowl, a glass dish with a goldfish swimming inside, rocks, a mirror, a metal box containing coins and a plunger, a fragment of Jan Van Eyck's Ghent altarpiece with coins lying in it, a rusting pistol, a coiled spring, paper, a torn calendar, a clockwork mechanism, and other detritus. The voice-over, which is occasionally spoken in a tone of uneasy laughter, gives way towards the end of the shot to the softly pulsating Indian-like electronic melody that has accompanied the opening credits. (Johnson and Petrie, p. 145)

As Kris Kelvin does in *Solaris*, Writer and Professor both reach the end of the film knowing a good deal more about themselves than they did at the beginning. The Strugatskys' Golden Ball has been changed in *Stalker* into a mysterious Room, in the middle of the Zone. This grants wishes to those who manage to reach its threshold, and who are sincere about their innermost desires. Writer and Professor want to visit the Room for different reasons:

Professor has set out to destroy it because he fears that evil people will put their wishes to maleficent use, and Writer seems to be in search of artistic inspiration. However, both men decide in the end not to enter the Room, apparently because some new degree of humility has enabled them to come to an acceptance of their flawed humanity and, at the same time, acknowledge something larger than themselves and their own needs. Tarkovsky comments that although outwardly 'their journey seems to end in fiasco, in fact each of the protagonists acquires something of inestimable value: faith' (*Sculpting in Time*, p. 199). In an exquisite shot – the last in the Zone itself, before the characters return to the bar from whence they began their journey – we see the three men, following their exhausting and frightening journey through the Zone's maze-like traps and terrors, sitting directly outside the fabled Room, looking in. Framed in golden light, rain suddenly starts to fall around them, apparently from inside the Room itself, glistening and shimmering in pools on the floor, and then, after several moments, ceases. Nobody moves, and the triptych of figures gradually fades out to black. Although the Room represents hope, redemption and salvation, this is evidently an ambiguous salvation, since neither of the two seekers, and certainly not Stalker (who we learn is forbidden to make wishes of his own: very different from the Red of the book) makes an overt attempt to claim it. Redemption, such as it is, seems to come in the form of acknowledgement that the Zone's mystery and inexplicability are to be revered, not exploited, and that some mysteries remain inviolable from the claims of human beings. The silence of Writer and Professor, in sharp contrast to their earlier argument and bickering throughout the journey, 'suggests a degree of respect and acceptance that is perhaps a form of prayer' (Johnson and Petrie, p. 147).

Stalker himself is one of the most memorable of all Tarkovsky's characters. He desires nothing for himself, and his motivation is to help those who are even more wretched and miserable than he is. These are the ones – not the rich, or the talented, or the famous – to whom the Zone opens its doors. Morally and spiritually robust, even as he recognises his own inadequacy and cowardice, Stalker epitomises a theological principle for the postmodern. In an age where faith and hope can seem to be meaningless obscurities, when all truths are relative, when all belief seems naïve, and when it seems as if there is nothing in the end left to hope for, there is – in what lies beyond his gaze, within the Room to which he faithfully leads those who truly are penitent at heart – a vision of something ineffable and eternal that remains real and meaningful, and which may finally effect transformation. In the beauty and reverence of its imagery, and the powerful lyricism of its thematics, Tarkovsky's vision of a world open to transcendence and hope remains unsurpassed by the dysphoric labyrinths of the Zone and *Stalker*, and is profoundly theological in the best sense of the word.

While science fiction seems to me to offer one of the most helpful frameworks for the dissemination of theological ideas, theology continues to emerge in the work of many film directors who are not engaged with this genre. Some of the most moving and theologically resonant reflections I can think of may be found in recent movies such as *American Beauty*, directed by Sam Mendes (1999), and Terrence Malick's extraordinary, extended meditation on war and comradeship, *The Thin Red Line* (1997). Both works explore at some length the nature and origin of 'beauty', and the transience and meaning of life. The same questions which have always preoccupied people are not going away just because the churches are not seen to be providing intelligible or attractive answers. Several current filmmakers are tackling hugely important and meaningful subjects in a manner with which people can richly identify. Several congregations in cinemas across the land are getting their spiritual fill from films that raise the most significant questions in language which is empathic and respectful, and which – since they are thoroughly grounded in the contexts of our own lives – offers a popular, memorable and authentic conceptuality. Robert K. Johnston is right when he says that 'If theology is boring to many (and that seems hardly controvertible), if one of the church's primary tasks is somehow to reconnect the church and contemporary life . . . if theology is wrongly absent from too much of public discourse – then movies might provide a means of reconnection' (*Reel Spirituality*, p. 97).

# CHAPTER 7

# Why Bother with Theology?

What I have tried to do in this short book is to identify some of the places where theology might usefully look for resources with which to counter the excesses of late western capitalism and secular postmodernity. This has involved an admission, along the way, that theology is generally perceived by outsiders to be tedious, irrelevant or anachronistic, and that these characteristics are related to the comprehensive marginalisation of Christianity and the Church at every level of our culture. Theology and Church are as disconnected from one another as are Church and society, and the consequence is that self-orientation, self-gratification and unfettered globalisation and consumption surge forward unchecked in our world, profoundly destructive at global, community and individual levels alike. What I have also tried to show is that in order to bring something to bear upon this situation which is not condescending, meaningless or otherwise out of touch, theology and the Church need to start with the world as it is – with the real situations of real people – before preaching to us about how it should be. Theology needs to get a life before telling us how to live ours. In the process of attempting this, I have looked at a number of representative theologies from Christian theologians who seem to me to have some integrity in their approach to existence in the twenty-first century. These theologies, while they differ in their specificities, are uniformly politicised, compassionate, socially engaged and responsibly communal. They are respectful, in a way that many other theologies are not, of the validity of life in the secular domain, even while they attempt to critique it. I have also examined some of the characteristics of what is known as the holistic movement, and have tried to identify some of the strands within that much-maligned galaxy which seem to me to be eminently credible and worth taking seriously. These include festivals out at the margins of respectability, such as Burning Man in Nevada, which re-energise and relocate Christian religiosity in some fascinating new ways. Finally, I have turned to a number of films and novels which seem to me to offer powerful repositories of theological wisdom, even though they are comprehensively grounded in secular settings.

What I have hoped to show is that theology has much to offer a culture which is obsessed with life in the here and now, but which – like the inhabitants of Ursula Le Guin's Earthsea – has relinquished its hold on what the value of that life means. The people of the *zeitgeist* have lost their bearings. This is the culture of the immediate – of mobile phones, virtual thrills, disposable commodities, different kinds of possessions, and above all of 'things', but at the expense of mature, reciprocal, responsible relationships conducted on terms other than the wholly self-absorbed. The paradox of self-gratification is that while taking away from others it simultaneously demeans and undermines the self. This results finally in an erasure of resources for everybody, so that the denial of the communal is but the prelude to the destruction of the individual. The myth of globalisation is that market forces enrich the many, but in effect the resources which should be of benefit to all are parcelled out by the rich and powerful to the already affluent and privileged (in other words, to their own constituencies) while the poor and undervalued struggle to get their share. Of course, in the end everybody loses: the world becomes more polluted, resources become scarcer and scarcer, global warming accelerates, and conflicts and betrayals over what few natural materials remain are the inevitable concomitant of this triumph of self-interest.

Theology's tragedy is that it has lost the authority it once had in challenging the dominance of the self. The institutions through which its directives were once commandingly articulated, the churches, are diminished or derided, or more likely are simply ignored. Theology and the Church have yet to face up to this fact, and its consequences, in any way that might be called visionary or convincing. Assuredly there are pockets of resistance. Individual theologians operate in their various ways with integrity and with some realistic sense of the crisis. Certain grass-roots Christian groups campaign effectively from the bottom up. But taken as a whole, the guild which is theology and the Church chooses to remain complacent, even though the statistics indicate that Christianity as it is presently understood and practised in the West will probably disappear in the next century. In the absence of a credible alternative to the principles and directives of the gospel texts, a veritable Babel of alternative spiritualities have filled the gap, with varying degrees of effectiveness, reliability and moral authority.

What, in this situation, is to be done? There are no easy answers. But there are pointers towards an alternative scenario which might prove rewarding to follow. In the first place, if theology were seen to be seriously engaged with other disciplines, in an effort to determine how they operate within the secular context, it might find for itself weapons to combat the deleterious imperatives with which the secular disciplines are so intimately familiar. Daniel Hardy, for one, is preoccupied with precisely this kind of recourse. In the second place, if theology were to move away from the rigidly hierarchical and liturgical structures which have characterised Christian worship for so long, but which now are heavily eroded, it might be able to validate areas of practice and belief which up to this point remain outside the boundaries of legitimate Christian life. In other words, theology might concentrate less on specific rites, such as the eucharist, or on doctrinal and credal formulations within the confines of church buildings, and focus to a greater degree on life outside of its recognised congregations. (For example, the ecumenical Taizé community in France succeeds in attracting thousands of people to its annual Christmas meeting in a manner that manages to transcend denominational and liturgical particularity.) As we have seen, an extraordinary richness of metaphysical and religious aspiration co-exists side by side with nominally secular culture, and urgently seeks means of effective articulation. In the third place, theology might return to an appreciation of its own narrative, and affirm its narrative as paradigmatic of the narratives of us all. The storytelling which we find in books and films offers – just as the parables of Jesus did – a potent critique of our leap towards self-combustion, whether this be directed towards ourselves as individuals or at the corporate and global level. In films like *The Matrix* we see the apparently unbeatable forces of corporate power overcome by a messianic figure and his followers, while in *Blade Runner*, despite the cacophony of confusions and disorientations in the post-modern Los Angeles, there is an acknowledgement of ultimate meaning and hope. In these cinematic texts, just as in the particular books I have discussed, we experience Tolkien's notion of 'Recovery'. Not only do we experience things as we were meant to see them, but we are offered a real sense of what lies beyond them, in – as *Blade Runner* envisages at one point – 'a golden land of opportunity and adventure'.

What, then, might theology in this land look like? It might be the lifeblood of a reverential approach to life which takes full account of the needs of the many as opposed to the few. It might utilise resources from within that very secular world in which it is placed, and relate to that world as co-explorer, partner and friend. It might move away from the rigidities of institutional worship towards fresh, and more fluid, modes of religious and liturgical expression, located within newly constituted and loosely federated groups of like-minded truth-seekers, Christian activists and godfearers. Its worship might be oriented less towards the doctrinal certainties of previous generations, and more towards the moral and ethical imperatives of the gospel stories, as those who seek illumination – today's disenfranchised and dispossessed – turn to the example of one who himself came as liberator of the lost. For all its adversities, selfishnesses and superficialities, British culture is impressively vibrant and influential and unexpected: and therein lies hope for our theology's salvation. For as Miranda Sawyer quite rightly says, 'We may turn ourselves into interesting statistics, we may conform to fascinating rules. But, truly, what we're best at is being the exceptions that prove them' ('Don't Fence Us In', *Britain Uncovered*).

The situation that I have described in this book, while frightening for churchpeople and theologians, is, as I see it, the reality. Because this is such a desperate scenario, it is probable that my evaluation will be attacked in certain quarters, not least because it straightforwardly acknowledges the challenge that is posed to the Church's survival, and is therefore profoundly threatening to the status quo. It is perhaps more comforting to dismiss the experienced reality of decline as cynicism or pessimism – or as the manifestation of a desire to promulgate, for one's own reasons, what is described as the 'secularisation thesis' – than to concur that the Church and its theology are in danger of being beached. Furthermore, a number of evangelical theologians discern in movements such as the Alpha Course compelling evidence that God's spirit is at work with a view to the mass conversion and reappropriation of the secular lost. By no means everybody will agree with the picture I paint here. It may well be dismissed in some circles as just another case of reheated liberalism, or as a further misguided attempt to accommodate Christianity and theology to the world on the world's terms rather than – as ought to be the case – on their own. It must be recognised that the theologians who describe themselves, or who have come to be described, as 'post-liberal' would wholeheartedly reject the presumptions that I make about where theology needs to go from here, and it is worth enquiring for a moment about the position that they might put forward instead.

The best-known and most influential proponent of post-liberal theology unquestionably is Stanley Hauerwas, Professor of Theological Ethics at Duke University, who in influential books such as *After Christendom?* (1991) and *Against the Nations* (1992), as well as in his more recent writings, has consistently rejected the notion that theology needs to find resources from secular culture in order to become more relevant or comprehensible. For Hauerwas, theology 'is best done without apology' (*Wilderness Wanderings*, p. 1), while in his own position he discerns a thoroughgoing attempt to explore 'how Christian claims about the world truly and truthfully display the way things are'. Such an exploration necessitates the rejection of liberalism on the grounds that finally it is morally incoherent; that talk about consensus and pluralism is in the end nothing more than rhetoric; and that an ethics which is divorced from 'a better hope' for the salvation which comes through discipleship to Christ's Kingdom is irredeemably compromised and ineffectual. For Hauerwas, as for many of his followers, the task of theology is decidedly not to become more empathic with the world in order to be seen to be relevant, but rather to show the world how to be authentically Christian. The Church, in other words, is the world's salvation. At the heart of this programme is a profound philosophical mistrust about language, or suspicion that one kind of discourse can necessarily be translated coherently into another kind. Hauerwas writes about this as follows:

> The notion that Christian speech can or must be translated if it is to be acceptable to modern people too often embodies simplistic views regarding the nature of language. For instance, such views of the linguistic character of the theological task fail to understand that the theologian should be trained as an adequate, skilful speaker of a language. From my perspective, if Christian theological claims are no longer doing any work, they are best given up, for it is far better to abandon such futile endeavours than subject them to a resurfacing operation (a 'face lift') that tries to show that they really mean something else. (*Wilderness Wanderings*, p. 3)

Elsewhere Hauerwas cites the emphasis placed (by the philosopher Alasdair MacIntyre) on the inarticulacy prevalent at the time of the Vietnam conflict as evidence that, despite so much being said at the time about the war, 'we were not able to speak intelligibly to each other on matters that were so deep' (*A Better Hope*, p. 32). According to this picture, the liberal language of consensus is in fact a rhetoric of emptiness, futile and hollow, which invites Christianity to fill its empty space.

Views such as this have led Hauerwas to be branded by liberal theologians as sectarian and divisive. On the face of it his positions might indeed seem suggestive of the sort of introversion characteristic of that placebo theology which puts Church before world at whatever the cost. However, Hauerwas is interesting and important because, despite his rejection of pluralism and liberalism – especially political liberalism – there is, paradoxically, a certain inclusiveness in his theology which goes beyond mere tribalism. As Hauerwas says, he has never sought 'to justify Christian withdrawal from social and political involvement'. He has merely wanted us 'to be involved as Christians' (*A Better Hope*, p. 24). There is a humility about Hauerwas' theologising which offers non-Christians, whether non-believers or those of other faiths, a space where moral authority might be recovered, and which involves a recognition that Christians are no better than anyone else ('Given the cosmic struggle Christians believe took place in cross and resurrection, the idea that its significance can be reduced to who is "better" belittles both God and those of us who struggle to worship and obey God', *Wilderness Wanderings*, p. 2). Similarly, his search for a voice which 'compels without coercion and persuades without denigration' posits a theology which 'cannot be enclosed', and which must not be afraid to 'discover itself still in the wilderness' (ibid.). This is all suggestive of a kind of theology that recognises its own limitations and is able – at least under certain conditions – to own up to its own mistakes.

Where I believe Hauerwas is mistaken is in assuming that the Christian tradition is a given, and that the Church has a kind of special legitimacy which renders it somehow resistant to the most profound critique with regard to its own continuing authority. For Hauerwas everything begins and ends with the Church as the guarantor of the cross and resurrection of Christ. There is a monolithic and breathtakingly self-assured aspect to this theology which starts with the doctrinal formulations and creeds, is endorsed and reinforced 'across the centuries and through the communion of saints' (*Wilderness Wanderings*, p. 5), and concludes with a recapitulation of traditional assertions. The fact that for a large number of people the Church and Christianity have no meaning or applicability to their lives is an indication not that the Christian tradition might have lost its way or its voice but rather that the Church needs to help the world 'discover that it is unintelligible just to the extent that it does not acknowledge the God we worship' (*A Better Hope*, p. 43). The consequence is that the experience of people from the bottom up, those multitudes of the unchurched and the Godless, is pushed to the outer rim of Hauerwas' universe. The point at issue is simply that their eyes need to be opened to the truth, and the truth will set them free, regardless of what they themselves may think or feel about the matter. Despite its welcome inclusiveness (at least in the sense that it is open to all) and prudent caveats about the provisionality of liberal strategies, such theology is at bottom deeply convinced of its own hegemony. It operates with the power and conviction which derive from a belief that the universe is black and white, and that it is on the side of the angels. For me it is reminiscent of one half of the debate in the British Conservative Party, which after defeat in the 2001 general election determined that the reason it was not electable was because it was not right-wing enough, and was perceived to have abandoned the core values by which it was customarily measured. Such reasoning, despite its rigidity, has a certain internal consistency, but it functions independently of the decisions made by large swathes of voters who have shifted fundamentally towards notions of plurality, liberalism and tolerance which are at odds with the traditionalism of so-called 'Tory values'. Unfortunately, if theology doesn't listen to the constituencies that it serves, and if churchpeople don't understand that they are massively out of touch with the secular thinking of people at large in our towns, cities and countryside, then they will remain as marginalised as those politicians who are widely perceived to be 'in it only for themselves'. Jane Shilling rightly recognises that, 'ashamed of its past and uncertain of its future, the established Church lacks both authority and charm. It is, in short, a thoroughly mediocre product – and the truth about mediocre products is that you can advertise them as hard as you like but the punters still won't buy them' (*The Times*, 3 September 2001).

So why bother at all, then, with theology? Because I believe that, despite its deficiencies, it is still able at its best to articulate that sense of the ineffable and essential which gives meaning, purpose and definition to our lives, both as individuals and as the social creatures who owe it to ourselves to look after one another and the planet that succours and shelters us. Far from perfect, challenged on all sides by indifference, weighed down as it is with the burden of its own considerable limitations, it may yet point towards a context where human beings may be freer, more complete, and more fully apprised of the mystery which is at the heart of all mysteries, from which we emerge and to which in the end we return. The theology which I am looking for, and to which I have tried tentatively to point in this book, will be the sensitive language of a Christian community that is outward-looking, self-effacing and non-dogmatic. It will begin from experience, conduct a process of exchange with the world, and critique the mastery of institutions and the top-down pronouncements of Church hierarchies, as well as the superficialities of life in the postmodern zone. It will serve as the codex for a federation of fellow travellers on life's way. Those travellers are oriented towards their brothers and sisters in a spirit of hope, and engage with their siblings' anxiety and despondency, but they know that, like the trio of seekers on the threshold of Tarkovsky's Room, there is finally a place which goes beyond words, or creeds, or doctrine. It is offered to us – the wretched and sometimes the despairing – miraculously, in the form of grace, and by it we are transformed.

# Bibliography

Bloom, William, ed., *Holistic Revolution: The Essential Reader*, London, Allen Lane, 2000

Bowker, John, *The Meanings of Death*, Cambridge, CUP, 1992

Brown, Callum G., *The Death of Christian Britain: Understanding Secularisation, 1800–2000*, London, Routledge, 2001

Brown, Simon, *Essential Feng-Shui: Your Practical Guide to Health, Wealth and Happiness*, London, Ward Lock, 1999

Bucknell, Barbara J., *Ursula K. Le Guin*, New York, Frederick Ungar, 1981

Bukatman, Scott, *Blade Runner*, London, BFI Publishing, 1997

Carpenter, Humphrey, *The Inklings: C. S. Lewis, J. R. R. Tolkien, Charles Williams and Their Friends*, London, HarperCollins, 1997

Cohn, Nik, *Yes We Have No: Adventures in Other England*, London, Vintage, 1999

Davie, Grace, *Religion in Modern Europe: A Memory Mutates*, Oxford, OUP, 2000

Davis, Mike, *City of Quartz: Excavating the Future in Los Angeles*, New York, Vintage, 1992

De Botton, Alain, *The Consolations of Philosophy*, London, Penguin Books, 2001

Dick, Philip K., *Do Androids Dream of Electric Sheep?*, London, Millennium Books, 1999

Diski, Jenny, *Skating to Antarctica*, London, Granta Books, 1997

Duncan, Glen, *Love Remains*, London, Granta Books, 2000

Forrester, Duncan B., *On Human Worth: A Christian Vindication of Equality*, London, SCM, 2001

Fowles, John, *The Magus*, London, Pan Books, 1968

Gee, Maggie, *Where Are the Snows*, London, Abacus, 1992

Gibson, William, *Neuromancer*, London, Voyager, 1995

Gorringe, T. J., *The Education of Desire: Towards A Theology of the Senses*, London, SCM, 2001

*The Sign of Love: Reflections on the Eucharist*, London, SPCK, 1997

Graham, David John, 'The Uses of Film in Theology', *Explorations in Theology and Film: Movies and Meaning*, eds. Clive Marsh and Gaye Ortiz, Oxford, Blackwell, 1997

Hardy, Daniel W., *Finding the Church: The Dynamic Truth of Anglicanism*, London, SCM, 2001

Harrison, Andrew, 'New Adventures in Sci-Fi', *Neon*, July 1997

Harvey, David, *The Condition of Postmodernity: An Enquiry into the Origin of Cultural Change*, Oxford, Blackwell, 1990

Hauerwas, Stanley M., *After Christendom?: How the Church is to Behave if Freedom, Justice, and a Christian Nation are Bad Ideas*, Nashville, Abingdon Press, 1991

*Against the Nations: War and Survival in a Liberal Society*, Notre Dame, University of Notre Dame Press, 1992

*A Better Hope: Resources for a Church Confronting Capitalism, Democracy, and Postmodernity*, Grand Rapids, Brazos Press, 2000

*Wilderness Wanderings: Probing Twentieth-Century Theology and Philosophy*, Boulder, Westview Press, 1997

Holden, Anthony, 'What Was Di For?', London, *Observer Review*, 10 June 2001

Holloway, Richard, 'Mixed Bathing in the Sea of Faith', *Time and Tide: Sea of Faith Beyond the Millennium*, eds. Teresa Wallace, Peter Fisher, Helen Fisher, Michael Elliott and David Hart, Alresford, O Books, 2001

Hunt, Stephen, *Anyone For Alpha?: Evangelism in a Post-Christian Society*, London, Darton, Longman & Todd, 2001

James, P. D., *Time to Be in Earnest: A Fragment of Autobiography*, London, Faber & Faber, 1999

Jameson, Fredric, *Postmodernism: Or the Cultural Logic of Late Capitalism*, Durham, Duke University Press, 1991

Johnson, Vida T. and Petrie, Graham, *The Films of Andrei Tarkovsky: A Visual Fugue*, Bloomington, Indiana University Press, 1994

Johnston, Robert K., *Reel Spirituality: Theology and Film in Dialogue*, Grand Rapids, Baker Academic, 2000

Kerr, Fergus, *Immortal Longings: Versions of Transcending Humanity*, London, SPCK, 1997

King, Geoff and Krzwinska, Tanya, *Science Fiction Cinema: From Outerspace to Cyberspace*, London, Wallflower, 2000

Kocher, Paul, *Master of Middle-Earth: The Achievement of J. R. R. Tolkien*, London, Penguin Books, 1974

Kundera, Milan, *Immortality*, trans. Peter Kussi, London, Faber & Faber, 1991

Leech, Kenneth, *The Eye of the Storm: Spiritual Resources for the Pursuit of Justice*, London, Darton, Longman & Todd, 1992

Le Guin, Ursula K., *The Farthest Shore*, London, Victor Gollancz, 1973

*The Left Hand of Darkness*, London, Futura, 1981

Lem, Stanislaw, *Solaris*, trans. Joanna Kilmartin and Steve Cox, London, Faber & Faber, 1970

Loughlin, Gerard, *Alien Sex: The Body and Desire in Cinema and Theology*, Oxford, Blackwell, 2002

'Ending Sex', *Sex These Days: Essays on Theology, Sexuality and Society*, eds. Jon Davis and Gerard Loughlin, Sheffield, Sheffield Academic Press, 1997

*Telling God's Story: Bible, Church and Narrative Theology*, Cambridge, CUP, 1996

Lovelock, J. E., *Gaia: A New Look at Life on Earth*, Oxford, OUP, 1979

Luhrmann, Tanya, *Persuasions of the Witch's Craft: Ritual Magic and Witchcraft in Present-day England*, Oxford, Blackwell, 1989

McCarthy, David Matzko, *Sex and Love in the Home: A Theology of the Household*, London, SCM, 2001

McFadyen, Alistair, *Bound to Sin: Abuse, Holocaust and the Christian Doctrine of Sin*, Cambridge, CUP, 2000

McFague, Sallie, *Speaking in Parables: A Study in Metaphor and Theology*, London, SCM, 1975

Mantel, Hilary, *A Change of Climate*, London, Penguin Books, 1995

Milbank, John, *Theology and Social Theory: Beyond Secular Reason*, Oxford, Blackwell, 1988

Milbank, John, Pickstock, Catherine and Ward, Graham, eds., *Radical Orthodoxy: A New Theology*, London, Routledge, 1997

Moltmann, Jürgen, *The Crucified God*, London, SCM, 1974

Monk, Ray, *Bertrand Russell: The Spirit of Solitude*, London, Jonathan Cape, 1996

Pattison, Stephen, 'Public Theology: A Polemical Epilogue', *Political Theology*, Sheffield, Sheffield Academic Press, May 2000

Pickstock, Catherine, *After Writing: On the Liturgical Consummation of Philosophy*, Oxford, Blackwell, 1997

Priest, Christopher, *The Extremes*, London, Simon & Schuster, 1998

*The Glamour*, London, Jonathan Cape, 1984

Redfield, James, *The Celestine Prophecy: An Adventure*, London, Bantam Books, 1994

Reilly, R. J., *Romantic Religion: A Study of Barfield, Lewis, Williams and Tolkien*, Athens, University of Georgia, 1971

Rilke, Rainer Maria, *The Selected Poetry of Rainer Maria Rilke*, ed. and trans. Stephen Mitchell, New York, Vintage, 1989

Ronson, Jon, *Them: Adventures With Extremists*, London, Picador, 2001

Russell, Bertrand, *Why I am Not a Christian*, London, George Allen & Unwin, 1975

Sammon, Paul, *Future Noir: The Making of Blade Runner*, New York, HarperCollins, 1996

Sawyer, Miranda, 'Don't Fence Us In', *Britain Uncovered*, London, *Observer Special Supplement*, 18 March 2001

*Park and Ride: Adventures in Suburbia*, London, Abacus Books, 2000

Selby, Peter, *Grace and Mortgage: The Language of Faith and the Debt of the World*, London, Darton, Longman & Todd, 1997

Sheldrake, Philip, *Spaces for the Sacred: Place, Memory and Identity*, London, SCM, 2001

Shilling, Jane, 'Riven by Ugly Squabbles, Ashamed of its Past and Uncertain of its Future, the Church is a Thoroughly Mediocre Product', London, *Times*, 3 September 2001

Strugatsky, Arkady and Boris, *Roadside Picnic*, trans. Antonina W. Bouis, London, Victor Gollancz, 2000

Tarkovsky, Andrei, *Sculpting in Time: Reflections on the Cinema*, trans. Kitty Hunter-Blair, London, The Bodley Head, 1986

Thubron, Colin, *Falling*, London, Penguin Books, 1990

Tolkien, J. R. R., 'On Fairy-Stories', *Tree and Leaf, Smith of Wootton Major, The Homecoming of Beorhtnoth*, London, George Allen & Unwin, 1975

*The Lord of the Rings*, London, George Allen & Unwin de luxe edition, 1969

Ward, Graham, *Cities of God*, London, Routledge, 2000

Weger, Karl-Heinz, *Karl Rahner: An Introduction to His Theology*, London, Burns & Oates, 1980

Weil, Simone, *Waiting for God*, New York, Harper & Row, 1973

Wieners, Brad, ed., *Burning Man*, San Francisco, HardWired Books, 1997

Williams, Rowan, *On Christian Theology*, Oxford, Blackwell, 1999

Winton, Tim, *The Riders*, London, Picador, 1995

Wray, Matt, 'Burning Man', *Bad Subjects*, 21, September 1995, University of California, Berkeley

Yates, Robert, ed., *Britain Uncovered*, London, *Observer Special Supplement*, 18 March 2001

Žižek, Slavoj, *The Fragile Absolute: Or, Why is the Christian Legacy Worth Fighting For?*, London, Verso, 2000

*The Plague of Fantasies*, London, Verso, 1997

# Index